SPIRIT
of LIFE

WILLIE SEALS

Copyright © 2024 Willie Seals.

All rights reserved. No part of this book may be reproduced, stored, or transmitted by any means—whether auditory, graphic, mechanical, or electronic—without written permission of both publisher and author, except in the case of brief excerpts used in critical articles and reviews. Unauthorized reproduction of any part of this work is illegal and is punishable by law.

ISBN: 979-8-89419-001-3 (sc)
ISBN: 979-8-89419-002-0 (hc)
ISBN: 979-8-89419-003-7 (e)

Because of the dynamic nature of the Internet, any web addresses or links contained in this book may have changed since publication and may no longer be valid. The views expressed in this work are solely those of the author and do not necessarily reflect the views of the publisher, and the publisher hereby disclaims any responsibility for them.

One Galleria Blvd., Suite 1900, Metairie, LA 70001
(504) 702-6708

CONTENTS

A New Spirit 1
A Person of Excellence 2
Abusiveness 4
Accept 6
Acceptance 7
Action 8
Affirmation 9
Alone 10
Ambition 11
Anticipation 12
Attitude 13
Awareness 14
Bad Decisions 15
Barrier to God 16
Be Grateful 17
Be Glad About Life 18
Be Happy 19
Beginning 20
Beginnings 21
Being Cheerful 22
Belief 23
Better! 24
Belonging 25
Believers 26
Be Good 28
Best 29
Blame 30
Blessed 31
Boldness 32

Built to Last! 33
Call on Him! 34
Change 35
Calling 36
Celebrate 37
Calm 38
Change 39
Change 40
Character 41
Choice 42
Character 44
Charismatic 45
Comfort Zone 46
Compassion 47
Competence 48
Complaining 49
Change Your Future 50
Consistently 51
Cheerful Giver 52
Clarity 53
Commitment 55
Creation 56
Confidence 57
Consciousness 58
Connected 59
Consent 60
Consequences 61
Control Your Mind! 62
Courage 63
Courage 64
Create 65
Creativity 66
Contentment 67

Cordial	68
Daring	69
Darkness	70
Deceitfulness	71
Deaf Ear	73
Decision	75
Do You Have Faith in People or God?	76
Deep Breath	77
Decisions	78
Devotion	79
Deceitfulness	80
Different	82
Direction	83
Discipline	84
Division	85
Diversity	86
Do it Now!	87
Don't Give Up On Me	88
Education	89
Elderly	90
Elevate	91
Empathy	92
Effort	93
Easy	95
Empower	97
Empowerment	98
Endure	99
Enjoyment	100
Enough	101
Expectations	102
Eyes Wide Open	103
Fantastic	104
Fellowship	105

Fertilize	106
Fight	107
Friends	108
Family Values	110
Focus	112
Follow your Heart	113
Free Will	114
Fresh Start	115
Frustration	116
Gift to Gab	117
Greatfulness	118
Go for it	119
Going Through	120
Good People!	121
Give Thanks	122
Growing	123
Grace	125
Guilty by Association	126
Grit	128
Heart	129
Happiness	130
Home Training	131
Helpfulness	133
Human	134
Humor	135
I Am	136
I am	137
I Think	138
I Will Try	139
I'm Gonna	140
Impactful Life	141
I am Going to Try	142
Insight	144

Instincts 145
Intention 146
Intuition... 147
Invaluable 148
It's In You! 149
I Guess 150
It's You... 152
Joy.. 153
Keep Your Energy! 154
Knowing Your Worth... 155
Keeping Your Word 156
Knowing Who You Are.. 157
Know 158
Knock Down 159
Laugh 160
Laws.. 161
Light of Hope 162
Life.. 163
Life.. 164
Lifting 165
Light 166
Lip Service 167
Love 168
Leaders... 169
Looking Forward Too.. 170
Looking Forward Too.. 171
Making Someone's Day Better 173
Manifesting.. 174
Meaningful Life!.. 175
Medicine 176
Mentoring.. 177
Merry! 178
Mind... 179

Mistakes	180
Music	181
New Ways!	182
Next Level!	183
Obedience	184
Options	185
Overcome	186
Overcoming	187
One of These Days!	188
Passing By	189
Patience	190
Peace	191
Persistence	192
Perspective	193
Planning	194
Powerful	195
Possessions	196
Power of Niceness	197
Powerless	198
Practice What You Preach	199
Prosperity	200
Peace of Mind	201
Pride	203
Purpose	205
Quest	206
Racism	208
Reflection	210
Relentless	211
Right Energy	212
Royalty	213
Right Perspective	214
Satisfied	215
Set Back	216

See Life 217
Seek God First 218
Self Mastery 219
Service 220
Servant 221
Shining 222
Small 223
Smile 224
Smile 225
Spirituality 226
Stand Out 227
Stand Up 228
Strength 229
Strong Faith 230
Succession 232
Surrender 233
Sustaining Love 234
Strength 235
Skills 236
Stand Still 238
Safe Haven 239
Time 241
Target 243
True Friend 244
The Hard Way! 245
Think 246
Thoughts 247
Together 248
Tolerance 249
Transformation 250
Truth 251
Tell Somebody 252
Testing 253

Thankfulness	254
The Spirit of Self Doubt	255
Unforgettable	257
Unique	258
Value of Life!	259
Vibrations	260
Victorious!	261
Voice	262
Wake up!	263
Walk Your Talk	264
Warrior	265
What about	266
What You Desire	267
What You Do With Your Time?	268
Who Am I	269
Willing to Act	270
Winning	271
Wisdom	272
Why	273
Waiting	274
What If	275
Who has Say over Your Life?	276
Who am I	278
Well Done	280
What You Care About?	282
Warriors For God	283
Your Must	284
Your Soul	285

Spirit

A NEW SPIRIT

....

Don't wish it was easier wish you were better. Don't wish for less problems, wish for more skills. Don't wish for less challenge, wish for more wisdom. The more we work on our own selves, the more our circumstances, and over all lives change the more we grow, and invest in ourselves. The more we will see a transformation, especially how we better communicate with others. When people think of having a positive attitude they might think that means showing surface level signs of happiness like putting a smile on one's face or trying to think happy thoughts. A positive attitude is something that goes deeper, and has an effect beyond surface cheer. Negative attitudes promote fear, while positive attitude do the opposite, and promote a more hopeful outlook on life. One of the greatest turning point in your life, and faith is when you realize you don't have to live life off reaction. Meaning when you speak your words are favorably received. No longer you need to let people and circumstances dictate the inner joy of your heart, leaving you wounded by someone's words or actions let the old go. Forgiveness stems from deep faith that we are enough that love abundant, and that even though we have been wronged we don't have to spend our emotional energy trying to have debt paid back to us. It takes practice to train our minds to learn to let go of what's not important so we can make room for things that really matter. Forgiveness is here to offer a place for people to come together, and focus on ways to learn to accept forgive, and love each other.

Head Shepherd
P.O.G.
Loving Ministry

Spirit
A PERSON OF EXCELLENCE

....

Job 37:23 Touching the almighty, we cannot find him out. He is excellent in power, and in judgment, and in plenty of justice: he will not afflict.

Good morning people of god. We as people of god must be people of excellence. So others will know what Jesus is about. It is hard sometimes because others will try to take advantage of us. Excellent people exceed expectations. In other words, they go the extra mile, they do more than what is asked.

If people were to describe your work, will excellence come to mind or simply mediocrity? Going above and beyond the call of duty takes conscious effort. Whatever you do in work or deed, do it all in the name of the lord Jesus, Whatever you do work at it with all your heart, as working for the lord, not for man since you know you will receive an inheritance from the lord as a reward.

We are called to strive for excellence in order to be the best testimony for the lord that we can be. Non- people of god are watching to see what kind of a difference that Jesus is making in your life and can point others to him by being diligent in your task and then above reproach in your ethics.

Excellence does not necessarily mean the absence of mistake, but it does mean the presence of faith and determination. To be excellent in whatever god has called you to do, you must first ask for his strength to accomplish the task, and then secondly, his endurance to complete it.

You must also recognize that there is a difference between striving to be perfect versus endeavoring to be excellent. Achieving perfection is an impossible task, because it never makes allowance for errors or mistakes. A person who strives for excellence does not give up when he makes mistakes. He does not avoid tasks for fear of failure. Do not think of today's failure but of the success that may come tomorrow. You will succeed if you persevere, and you will feel joy in overcoming obstacles.

Remember No efforts we make to obtain something beautiful is ever lost. The true goal of excellence is do the best you can with what you have with every moment. Whatever you are / be all there. Make it yours, period.

Head Shepherd
POG
Loving Ministry

Spirit ABUSIVENESS

Judges19:25 But the men would not hearken to him: so the man took his concubine, and brought her forth unto them, and they knew her and abused her all the night until the morning, and when the day began to spring, they let her go.

Good Morning People of God. Men, you do not have to beat your lady to make her feel afraid to leave you. Just treat her like a queen who she is by showing love and respect for her with all your heart. You are not training a dog to obey you, but your woman is a part of you. If she is hurting then you are hurting too. God created woman so man would have someone to show his love to. When you hit a lady you make her feel less than herself. When you take away her self-esteem she is no longer a person.

When you yell at her and talk bad about her, it is like you are hitting her. So speak with words of inspiration to her and be uplifting. Abusiveness is a form of slavery to keep a person in check. When a slave didn't do what the master wanted him to do they beat them with the whip. So people, do we really need to hurt someone if we say we love them?

Of course not, so don't. Our ways should be like Jesus' ways. Always showing love and caring for one another. Abusiveness is just another trait of the devil. Remember he wants us to rob, kill, and destroy each other.

More than one in 10 high school students have already experienced some type of physical aggressiveness from a dating partner. And more of these teens do not know what to do when it happens. Sometimes abusive behavior does not cause pain or even leave a physical bruise, but it is still unhealthy.

Some signs of abuse are putting you down, explosive tempers, mood swings, and checking your cell phone without your permission.

Always aim to show kindness and do good to one another and to everybody you meet. We ought to love our enemies. We are to do good to them that spitefully use us. Evil is never overcome by more evil but goodness will always win in the end.

Love should overlook a person's flaws.

Head Shepherd
POG
Loving Ministry

Spirit
ACCEPT

Romans 14 The weak and the strong. Accept the one whose faith is weak, with out quarreling over disputable matters. One person's faith allows them to eat anything, but another, whose faith is weak, eats only vegetables. The one who eats everything must not treat with contempt the one who does not, and the one who does not eat everything must not judge the one who does, for God has accepted them.

Good morning people of God. There comes a time in our lives when you have to accept some things. There are all kinds of reasons why you must accept somethings. Like your older now your body does not work like it use too, and it seems like it is too late. We want to start a family at a time, but now the biological clock has run out. We want the perfect body, and now joint pains has set in. it is so hard for us to accept these things in life. We have been trying all our lives to make something good happen for us. Time is not on our side, it is something you cannot get back. Accept there are some things you cannot do. God has given you a gift find that gift. When you know what you are good at in life. Do it with all of your heart. That is your purpose in life. Let go and let God. Stop living your life all frustrated about something you can't do. Have faith in God he knows what you should be doing in life. Accept your limitations we all can't do the same thing in life. Your heavenly father accept you in your sinning ways. So accept him so he can deliver you from your sinning ways.

Head Shepherd
P.O.G.
Loving Ministry

Spirit
ACCEPTANCE

....

1 Timothy 1:15 Here is a trustworthy saying that deserves full acceptance. Jesus came into the world to save sinners of whom I am the worst.

Good morning people of God. People in society today are so concern about others accepting them. They will go through great lengths trying to be someone who they are not just to be accepted by others. We must learn that all people are not like you. Even Jesus could not make everyone like him. And see what they did to him. Accepting ourselves unconditionally is difficult because, we must give up the fantasy that if we punish ourselves enough with negative thoughts, we will change. Its as if we can whip ourselves into shape saying things like. There is something wrong with me if I didn't have lots of friends,and an active social life,but as I have learned from experience this strategy doesn't work. In fact the more anxious we become. The frighten little child does not respond favorably to such a mean. Dictator instead we need to find ways to accept the anxious part of ourselves, to hold that part by the hand and gently say you OK. Remember acceptance does not mean you have given up, and not trying anymore. In contrast it means your looking at yourself and your situation realistically. Of course there are aspects of my life I want to work on. I am always trying to be a better person. But as I keep relearning its easier to work towards change if I am not wasting energy criticizing myself for perceived flaws. Just remember God loves you for who you are. He has placed a gift in you so you can be that person he created you to be in short just love your self and love others.

Head Shepherd
P.O.G.
Loving Ministry

Spirit
ACTION

. . . .

Psalm 33:15 He is the one who transform the human heart, and takes note of all their actions.

Good morning people of God. We as people of God must start putting some action behind our faith. We must show other people that God can do all things when you ask him and put some action with it. People of God are always talking about how good God is. But not all the time showing others how good he is with some action. Like doing for others, helping others, caring for other, and sharing. We must start these things so we can grow the kingdom of God. There is a whole lot of lip service out there already. People of God must be about the actions so others can see God is real and start believing in him and his son Jesus. Because action speaks louder than words and People will see we are doers and not Sayers. With God with us there is nothing we cannot do. All things are possible with Christ! Let's stop waiting to see if others will show love first we the people of God will be first. Action is hard to do, but with a positive mind and prayer you can take the first step of faith. Be about doing the work of God loving, Caring, and sharing with others. Focusing on the cost of action and on the pleasures of in action demotivates them from acting to bring themselves long range happiness you want to reverse this by using cost, and benefit to your advantage. What you want to do is focus both on the benefit of following through on your happiness action plan, and the cost of in action. If you keep clear about the benefit of doing and the cost of not doing you strengthen your commitment to act.

Head Shepherd
P.O.G.

Spirit AFFIRMATION

1 John 5:13 I write these things to you who believe in the name of the son of God so that you may know that you have eternal life.

The action or process of affirming something or being affirmed. Why can't we be people of emotional support or encouragement to each other. We are so quickly to tear each other down and not build-up. It takes more energy to smile then to frown. Why is it so hard to compliment someone. We all need that positive feedback. Be that person with words of encouragement. If we as people can always have something nice to say about each other, then this world will be a beautiful place. You can attract more bees with honey than with vinegar. Be that light of hope always looking to put a smile on someone face. When your nice to someone they will always want to be there for you. Love attract love like hate attracts hate simple right! When we are able to have compassion for each other it makes life much peaceful. When you see someone doing what is right be the 1st one to compliment them. Tell them job we'll done my friend. People love to hear something positive about their life. Be that coach of inspiration always uplifting. If we truly want to change this world. We must start letting each other know what we mean to one another. Don't be afraid to give someone a compliment. Tell them how much they mean to you. God so loved the world. He gave his son so you would have everlasting life.

Head Shepherd
P.O.G
Loving Ministry

Spirit
ALONE

T he universal God will never leave you alone. You must knock and the door shall be open. Stop living a selfish life. Trying to do everything yourself. People believe that spending time alone can be good for creativity, self insight, self development, relaxation, and spirituality. One if the most important determinate of whether time alone is a good experience or a fought one is whether you choose to be alone. If you want to create a new personal life reality a new life we must begin to examine the thoughts, emotions, and behaviors we've been living by and change them. People who are lonely feel Isolated, and think that no one is interested in them on their lives. So they often push people away. Don't fall into this trap. Work places are sometimes subject to cliques, but that does not mean the cliques won't be interested in letting you in, if you show interest. As the saying goes no man is an island your not going to achieve any measurable success if you try to go it alone. People love compliments it is human nature. Find genuine reason to give compliments to others. Giving other people positive feedback, about their selves open them up to you. They are more likely to form friendships With you and to return the favor of positive feedback. Friendships are built brick by brick people are not born with your friends that will develop over time, and shared experiences. Deturonomy chapter 31 verse 6 it lets you know that you should be courageous and no you are not alone Since the Lord God is always with you.

Head Shepherd
P.O.G.
Loving Ministry

Spirit
AMBITION

A strong desire to do, or to achieve something, typically requiring determination, and hard work. When we first start out on the path of life we are filled with ambition, to achieve the impossible. It seems like the world is our canvas to paint whatever we desire. We are filled with possibilities to achieve our dreams. Then the problems of life starts to set in to discourage us. The enemy knows if he can change your thoughts, he can destroy your world. Colossians 3:2 set your mind on the things that are above, not on the things that are on Earth. When you live by the words you will always rise above. The best way to stay ambitious is by looking at people around you working relentlessly toward their dreams, goals, and aspirations. If you want to achieve more you have to work hard with a single pointed concentration to, become a successful person. Your destiny fate should support you to achieve your dreams, and ambition we just accept our life the way it is, but it doesn't change the problem we face.. And one day we will regret for accepting the life as it is, and not fighting for the life we actually needed. God has placed a talent in each and every one of us. It is up to you to be able to manifest this talent. That you want and move forward with it in your life. Let go of who you think you are, so you can become who you truly are!

Head Shepherd
P.O.G.
Loving Ministry

Spirit

ANTICIPATION

Proverbs 3:5-6 Trust in the Lord with all thine heart, and lean not unto thine own understanding. In all thy ways acknowledge him, and he shall direct thy path.

Good morning people of God. Why is it that people go through life waiting for something good to happen for them? Hoping that things will turn out right. We must give God something to bless for you. Meaning that you must take some action, and put somethings in place that you want to do in life. It says in the bible faith with out action is dead. Whatever good you want out of life just have a way to achieve it. Your heavenly father wants you to have the good things in life. When you are doing good things for people, you can believe good things will happen to you. Your attitude must be positive all the time. Seeing your destiny being incredible. Take the leap of faith. Knowing your God is right there with you. You can have heaven on earth when you love yourself, and others. Your thoughts can transform the way you look at life. Loving, sharing, and caring, for others will always make your life a delight. Let your heart be filled with compassion for others. Be happy about life no matter what the enemy try to do to you. Know your father wants you to have a smile on your face. Paradise is with in you. Believe, and know this can happen for you. Your mind set is your power to defeat the enemy.

Head Shepherd
P.O.G.
Loving Ministry

Spirit
ATTITUDE

Ephesians 4:23 To be made new in the attitude of your minds.

If you want to change your life you must have an attitude of gratefulness. You must be able to be thankful for what God has done for you already then he will always give you more. We are like magnets you will attract what you want with your thoughts. It's vital that you have a positive attitude at all times. Pain or regret is so much worse than the pain of discipline. It's going to be hard but hard does not mean impossible. Don't let anyone tell you that you can not have a joyful heart. You must envision yourself being happy at all times. No matter what the situation is in life we must be able to reflect a good attitude in our behavior. A position of the body posture or implying an action or mental state. If you can try to stay away from negative thoughts in negative people in your life. If you change the way you look at things the things you look at change. Make a different in every one you meet in life. Show them that Christ has a purpose in life for them. Every time you keep a commitment to someone in life they will gain confidence in you, and listen to you when you share the word. When you truly believe in yourself everyone around you will feel the positive energy. When you have the Holy Spirit living in you all your thoughts become possible your mental state is your connection to the universal God stay filled with good cheer in love for humanity.

Head Shepherd
P.O.G.
Loving Ministry

AWARENESS

God only selects his greatest warriors for the hardest battles. Never give up the good fight. We live our lives with blinders on, and not seeing the world through our spiritual eyes. Not noticing all the things that are going on in the world. Just an our surrounding. We have to stop thinking of self, and consider others. In order to change this reality in this world just watched the sky and Be observant of all the events in the world. Earthquake, floods, snowstorm, and fires. Are all signs of what's about to come. If we as a people don't change our ways. We will be enslave by this enemy, and your freedoms will be taken away. Life Is hard but overcoming life is even harder. But when you start seeing the change that made it worth the fight. A life without a cause is a life without effect. Step out of your world of unawareness. Starts seeing the world thought your spiritual eyes, and see how much control this enemy really has. Are you aware of what is happening around you? Most people are too focused on themselves on their thoughts, desires or smartphone and are not. Really aware of what is happening around them. I rarely see people raising their head up, and looking at the moon or the stars. When was the last time you looked at the beautiful sky at night? Or notice how the moon looks on different nights? When was the last time you saw the sun setting or rising? I suggest that every now and then you stop what you are doing, and look at the world around you. The first step toward change is awareness the second step is acceptance then trying to make the situation better!

Head Shepherd
P.O.G.
Loving ministry

Spirit
BAD DECISIONS

John 8:16 If I do judge, my decisions are true because I am not alone. I stand with the father who sent me.

Good morning people of God. We as p.o.g. has all done something that we regret doing. A bad decision is all it was. Like hooking up with the wrong mate after everyone has told you they are no good for you, and now you are in an abusive relationship. Hanging with the wrong friends, and letting peer pressure get the best of you, and now you are hooked on drugs. Letting anger and hatred get the best of you and you take a life, and now your on death row. There are so many bad decisions people have made in life. Now you are not able to love yourself anymore feeling unworthy,of gods love. The enemy is hard at work daily putting the wrong thoughts in your head. You must be able to tell what is a good thought,or a wrong one. If there isn't no sin in the thought then it is the right one. Your a person of excellence just believe in yourself, and start loving again. God will not hold anything against you that you have done. Just ask your father to forgive my trespass, and those who have trespass against you. He loves you that much he will forgive you. When making a decision make sure you weigh the pros, and cons of different options. To begin to understand, and apply those insights, we must first start with a basic premise. That we don't always think about our choices, and decision the same way. Sometime we may think about things in more of a fast, and automatic way. And other times we may consider things more slowly, and deliberately. In turn each of these ways of making decisions has its own pros and cons. In short just remember when making a decision keep God in it, and your father will never let you be wrong.

Head Shepherd
P.O.G.
Loving Ministry

Spirit
BARRIER TO GOD

Proverbs 10:11 A person's wisdom yields patience it is to one's glory to overlook an offense.

Good morning people of God. Do you know what is stopping you from God glory? We wonder why we never hear from God. Its because of your sin's that whats keeping you away from him. Your mind and heart isn't pure the devil has a hold on you. In order for you to be close to God there must be love and compassion in your heart. You must be concerned about others well being. We as people are only concerned about ourselves. This isn't how God wants you to be. His son died so you may be free from the enemy. He showed you unselfish love with this act. We as people would never think about doing something like that. Yes his love is that great for you. We must feel like Christ and have love for others in that same way. When there is caring, sharing, and loving for others God will always listen to you. There will be nothing that he will not do for you what is right. Lets stop being blocked from Gods love. Take all the negative thoughts out of your mind. Believe in something greater by having thoughts of positivity. God will never not be there for you when you think like this. God is a positive spirit who work with the same energy. Whenever you are going through sad or bad God will turn it around to good or happy. He will not leave you in a depressed state. There is tremendous energy in Gods words you must read the book so you know how this works. Whatever you think that will be the state you will be in good or bad. You have the choice on how you want to feel.

Head Shepherd
P.O.G.
Loving Ministry

Spirit
BE GRATEFUL

....

Psalm 147:7 Sing to the Lord with grateful praise; make music to our God on the harp.

Good morning my p.o.g. family have you ever wondered why you are not getting what you want out of life? May be it is, because you are not grateful for what you have already. Stop taking for granted the car you have, and the house you live in. There are so many others who would love to be in your shoes. Your heavenly father wants you to be grateful for what he has given you already. Then he may just give you more. Be content with the little things then your father will know you will appreciate the big things in life. Say thank you when people do things for you, or give you something. Life is like a boomerang whatever you throw out there it surely will come back to you. Always have an attitude of just enjoying life. Be happy about where you are in life. When you are grateful for what life has given you. You will truly get more. Don't let the enemy deceive you believing that you shouldn't be thankful. Each and everyday wake up with the mind set of being grateful. Go out in the world being thankful for what all the Lord has done for you. Live life like this is your last day. Be joyful, and happy in every moment of your life. Life is too short for you not to be enjoying it. This is a day that the Lord has made.

Head Shepherd
P.O.G.
Loving Ministry

Spirit

BE GLAD ABOUT LIFE

To achieve excellence in your life is important to be willing to let go of anything that is not serving you. This may include negative thought patterns, toxic relationships, or unproductive habits. By taking a step back and you value waiting what truly brings value. and joy to your life, you can create space for excellence to flourish. It may be a difficult process, but the rewards of letting go of the mediocre and striving for excellence are worth it. Remember to be kind to yourself throughout this process, and stay focused on your dream. It seems like an odd question but is it? Do you know how to define glad? Do you think glad is the same thing to you as it is to others? What's the point of it all? Does it even make? A difference in our lives? And fact happiness does have a pretty important role in our lives, and it can have a huge impact on the way. We live our lives. When we are glad enough. Our most important relationship usually our spouse, or children, and our parents. Other close family members, and our closest friends. We tend to be glad. We have some control over how our? Relationships. Go, so that leads us to an interesting? And important Question. Can we be more glad in our life. Choose a position mantra for all the day. Something you will repeat to yourself such as today is beautiful or I feel great. and when things go South take a moment to try and see it from a positive light. Never underestimate the importance of recognizing the silver lining. In life. Keep doing your best so that your future will not be regret.

Head Shepherd
P.O.G
Loving Ministry

Spirit

BE HAPPY

Every major decision comes with a risk, and that's why people avoid them. If you Don't fail you don't learn if you don't learn you don't grow! We are not yesterday we are right now sometimes what's holding us back from happiness is our environment like being caged, and can't grow. That's why we should move out, and wander to find your purpose in life. Choices are here for us to make wise decisions on what you actually choosing. Everything happens for reason meaning no matter what path you choose will be what's destined you take. Just trust that path and continue to grow from your trials and tribulations. Don't compare yourself to others just be better than yourself each and every day. The next time you're having a bad day, or a negative reaction to something don't ignore your emotions to put on a smile. Instead try accepting the way you feel as a legitimate, and try to identify what you are feeling and why. By knowing who you are And what you stand for you come to life choices with the most powerful Tool of all your full self. This is much better way to choose happiness for yourself don't frown, because you never know who is falling in love with your smile. Believe in yourself you are braver than you think, and more talented than you know, and capable of more than you can imagine. You can't go back and change the beginning, but you can start where you are, and change the ending. Don't tell people about dreams show them your results be happy life is too short not to be.

Head Shepherd
P.O.G.
Loving Ministry

Spirit
BEGINNING

To all the believers out there don't ever let the world's negativity disenchant you or your spirit. If you surround yourself with love, and the right people anything is possible. The best time to get started is yesterday, the next best time is now, in the beginning God-created light so we may have abundance in life. But slowly the enemy changed the perception of the world. By tricking the believers to believe what is bad is right. We must change the way we see reality, and come back to the light. Beginning a new life can seem overwhelming at 1st. However with courage and determination you may find that starting over is an opportunity to make your life even better. Some personal tragedy may have destroyed your home, job, or relationship. Either way the 1st step in starting over is knowing what you want from life. Even if you are not happy With beginning a new life prioritizing what is important for you to do in the new life is helpful. Having clear goals and determining what you need to do to achieve them will help you feel more confident, and optimistic, about building your new life. Therefore if anyone is in Christ he is a new creation. The old one has passed away behold the new has come.

Head Shepherd
P.O.G.
Loving Ministry

Spirit
BEGINNINGS

Genesis 9 Gods covenant with Noah then God blessed Noah and his sons, saying to them," Be fruitful and increase in number and fill the earth. The fear and dread of you will fall on all the beasts of the earth, and on all the birds in the sky, on every creature that moves along the ground, and on all the fish in the sea; they are given into your hands. Everything that lives and moves about will be food for you. Just as I gave you green plants, I now give you everything.

It comes a time when you must begin to take steps to get what you want. Sitting on the sideline you will never cross the finish line. You will never have anything in life if you let one failure stop your dream. We will fall many times before you can walk. Life has many obstacles you must learn to navigate around them if you want to be successful. God says you must ask for what you want in life. Knock and the door will be open. You must 1st believe in yourself to achieve your goals. We are all are underdogs in life. We must learn to never give up the fight. When you are able to have clarity to your vision. It is about to be revealed to you. There will be times you will become weary just find strength to move on. When you are able to not let life difficulties affect You. That is when you are in control of your reality. You are able to create whatever environment You choose to exist in. Fill your mind with thoughts of greatness let the spirit lead you to your destiny in life. Let love guide you then there will be nothing you can't get through. Do onto others as you would have them do to you. Be grateful you have been given a chance to begin again.

Head Shepherd
P.O.G.
Loving Ministry

Spirit

BEING CHEERFUL

There will always be sad times in your life. The key is to not dwell on them. Choose to be cheerful no matter what happened in your life. You are the master over your emotion cheerfulness is special, because of how it affects others. It isn't just something that you feel on your own it involves expressing positive feelings. To those around you acting cheerful when you're really not happy can actually produce the opposite effect in those around you. You may think you are great at faking any emotions. But your body language and facial expressions can reveal your true feelings. By focusing on what you're passionate about, and learning to share the this passion with others you can become more cheerful you've got to follow your passion. You've got to figure out what it is that you love who you really are and have the courage to do that. I believe that the only courage anybody ever needs is the courage to follow your own heart. The comfort of your own knowing the clarity of your own knowing, because you are grateful. No matter what being grateful changes your personal Vibrations. Success is walking from failure to failure with no loss of enthusiasm. Try not to become a person of success, but rather try to become a person of value. The Secret of change is to focus all of your energy not on fighting the old but on building the new. Be happy no matter what, let people know you care about their life. Stay committed to your decisions but stay flexible in your approach.

Head Shepherd
P.O.G.
Loving Ministry

Spirit

BELIEF

Job 11:4 You say to God "My beliefs are flawless and I am pure in your sight."

Bad things happen when good people choose to do nothing. God has given us free will so choose to do right. Your mind is the most powerful transmitter in the world. It connects us directly to the universal God. That is why the enemy is trying so hard to control your perception about life. There are so many different beliefs in the spiritual realm. It is so critical that you keep watch over your mind, and what you believe in. Nothing in the world is so elusive yet so powerful as our beliefs. They have the power to dictate the direction of our lives for good or bad, and they seemingly come out of nowhere..Simply put they are developed as a child and stick with you like glue into adulthood. The larger question isn't which beliefs are right or wrong is how do our beliefs affect our lives? Are they having a positive impact or negative impact. We are spiritual beings who need to make a choice and live our lives for lives for God. Stop being of the world, and start doing what is right in life. Love yourself and others stop judging people. Want more for others than you want for yourself that is when you are living in God's reality. God said with lack of knowledge people will perish We must believe that the universal God has things in his control. Whatever outcome you want for your life you must first believe it, and be able to see it in your mind. Transform yourself from being a creation to being a creator.

Head Shepherd
P.O.G.
Loving Ministry

Spirit
BETTER!

John 5:14 And this is the confidence that we have in Him that if we ask anything according to his will he heareth us.

Good morning people of God. Why people in the world today do not like who they are? Because they don't feel that they can do better. Always trying to recreate themselves from who God created them to be. Believe in the ways of the world is what they should be. There will always be a better doctor, a better singer, a better athlete. Stop beating yourself up, and have confidence on who God created you to be. You was made in the image of the almighty God. There is no one like you in the world you're the only copy made. Meaning your unique and wonderfully made. There is no one better than you believe in yourself. Go out and take the world by storm. Be creative have great thoughts knowing that all things are possible. Whenever you want to do better in life speak words of positivity about yourself. Envision great accomplishments that you can do. Be bold, and courageous, There is nothing you cannot do because your heavenly father is with you.

Head Shepherd
P.O.G.
Loving Ministry

Spirit

BELONGING

Genesis 45:20 don't worry about your belongings, for the best of all the land of Egypt will be yours."

Good morning people of God. People in society today wants to belong to some type of group. We need acceptance of others to feel our self worth. We will go through great lengths to fit in where we think we should be. There are some people who will give up their customs, just to be like Mike. We are all made in the image of Christ. There are many different races of people. But in Gods eyes there are only two, and that is good and bad people. You need to figure out which one you belong to. If you break it down it can be as simple as positive or negative people it's that simple. The law of the universe says what you think is what you attract to yourself. Meaning if you are always thinking about bad things then that is what will happen to you. God is the same way if you do what he says, and do good to others he will have good things happen for you in your life. Belong to God click., and you will never be wrong about anything in life. Even all animals species run together not willing to hang around other animals. The deer with the deer the sheep with the sheep. Aren't we as people more evolved than animals and able to get to know different race of people? We are made in God's image meaning there is only one image. People we are all the same. So let's work together and make this world a better place. There is no reason trying to be different from whom God created you to be. People of loving, helping, sharing, and caring, about one another. Stop trying to fit in where you know you don't fit. God has a purpose for all of Gods' people. He wants you to belong to the kingdom of God and do his will. Membership in this Kingdom will give you privileges of power to do all things through Christ. WILL YOU JOIN TODAY!

Head Shepherd
P.O.G.
Loving Ministry

Spirit
BELIEVERS

Psalms 106:2 they believed his promises; they sang praise to him.

Good morning people of God. We as people of God must believe totally in the resurrection of Jesus Christ. With no doubt that this happened and be able to tell it with conviction. We stop ourselves sometime believing totally when things in life start going wrong. Then that is the time your faith must kick in and be stronger. We need to feed our spirit daily with the reading of the word. Then when doubt sets in we would be able to turn it off. The devil knows when your time of weakness is at its best. Then he will try to stop you from believing in Jesus Christ. Believers have faith that guides them through life. It's just sometime we let the battery get low. We need other believers around us whose battery is fully charged. Then they can help us recharge our battery again with the power of Gods words. We must believe that Jesus died but came back to life so we can have everlasting life. Through the ages man and woman were willing to die whether than believe this happened. Others have devoted their lives to explained how this happened, using the most advance scientific tools available,and delving into the most mind boggling theological to try to make since of it. Just believe and walk in faith then slowly God will start revealing things to you. We all go through life not knowing where it will lead us. That is believing in the father and the son knowing that when you walk in faith God will always lead you in the right path in life. Believing for something better in life should always be your first thoughts, and being grateful for what you have already in life. True believers know God is a positive energy always present in the air that you breathe. God is all around you just know he is and keep doing what is right in life by helping and loving others. When we believe them we are exercising our power to the name of God and bring into being a world we love that loves us, and by exercising this capacity we stir in ourselves the feelings of vitality, direction and belonging that our desire for spirit seeks as the conditions for our ongoing well being. It is intoxicating. We find ourselves believing and in whatever we perceive as enabling us to thrive. God is true because God lives in me enabling me to be who I am.

Head Shepherd
P.O.G.

BE GOOD

Chronicles 16:34 O give thanks unto the Lord, for he is God for his mercy endure forever.

Good morning people of God In a world today why is it so hard for people to be good to one another? It seems we would prefer to hate one another before being good to one another. God said that the end time will be filled with self love. The only one people can see being good to is themselves. Being good to someone shouldn't be so hard. Just smile, wave, or speak when you see someone. God has promised that when you are nice to someone nice things will happen for you. Be glad you are able to move about on your own strength. Be good to people who don't have, and be willing to share with them. Be good to your neighbor by trying to get to know them. We all need to be good people by trying to change our evil ways. Good is something so hard for some people to be. God is so good to you each and everyday. Good means a lack of self centeredness it means the ability to empathize with other people to feel compassion for them, and to put their needs before your own. It means if necessary, sacrificing your own well being for the sake of others, it means benevolence, altruism, and selflessness, and self sacrifice towards a greater cause- all qualities which stems from a sense of empathy, it means being able to see beyond the superficial difference of race, gender, or nationality, and relate to a common human essence beneath them.

Head Shepherd
P.O.G.
Loving Ministry

Spirit
BEST

....

2 Samuel be strong! Let's fight bravely for the sake of our people and the cities of our God! The Lord will do what he decides is best!

Good morning people of God. We as P.O.G. must always want to be and do our best in life. Others are watching us to see if they can see God in us. Be on your best behavior all the time. This will be difficult because the devil is hard at work 24 hrs a day. Being your best will start with your mind by training it to be happy all the time. When you feel good about what you are doing in life it is easy to be happy. Whatever you do make sure you are doing it to the best of your ability. If you are working the fry station be your best at it. Know that God has a bigger purpose for you in life. When you live life as a person of excellence God will always take care of you. Wake up each and every morning trying to be better than the day before. Then you will see the best is yet to come. Be positive about life and have a mind set of excellence. People will be hating on you for trying to be your best. Please do not let this discourage you. It is only the devil trying to keep you from Gods best. Most of us wish we could improve certain things about ourselves. Lasting change is difficult. Many of our habits are deeply ingrained, and certain core, personality attributes may be immutable. But even the oldest of habits and character traits can be altered into varying degrees, as it is never too late to change, with effort and determination; it is possible to be the person you want to be. Always put your best effort forward in life. When people see you at your best they know you are someone of importance. Child of God the most high!

Head Shepherd
P.O.G.
Loving Ministry

Spirit
BLAME

Deuteronomy 18:13 You must be blameless before the Lord your God.

Don't you think it's time to stop blaming people for your life situations? It's time you take accountability for your decisions you make. If no one's fault if you don't get the opportunities in life. God did not give you a spirit of doubt. When you are a true believer all things become possible fear of making mistakes is healthy. When it raises intensity motivates. perspiration and inspire vigilance. It's unhealthy when it paralyzes you give yourself reasonable time to explore options, and then take action. Stop letting others opinion define who you are. It's not about who you are today, it's about who you want to become, and the price your willing to pay to get there. All the bad decisions you made in your pass. Don't let it keep you from doing what's right today. In order to change your life. You must first stop letting people dictate to you the outcome of your life. turn off those outside voices, and just listen to God. When you take charge of your mind you are in control of your life. Stay focused and discipline to your desires. Never regret A-day in your life. Good day gives you joy, while a bad day gives you experience. Both are important for a blameless life.. You are loved by someone even if you feel alone. You are not alone and you are important to someone. Keep fighting a good fight of faith. Believe in your capabilities!

Head Shepherd
P.O.G.
Loving Ministry

Spirit
BLESSED

Proverbs 10:22 The blessing of the Lord brings wealth without painful toil for it.

Good morning people of God. We as P.O.G. are so blessed to have a God that loves us. Our heavenly father will do anything to take care of us. We need not to worry about nothing when we believe in him. The enemy will stay far away when the father is near. He sent his son Jesus to do the unthinkable, so that you will have everlasting life. If there was more people like this loving, caring about one another this will be a much better place. We are blessed and highly favored by our God. All things are possible with God! More wealth, better health, healing, and new beginnings there is nothing that God will not do for you when you follow his words. There is power in the resurrection of blood running through you. There is nothing you cannot do, there is nothing you cannot have. You have the control over how you want your life to be. Have a bigger vision about what you want to do in life. When your vision consist of helping others God is there with you. God has made the blind see the lame walk. And risen Jesus from the dead. There is nothing that he will not do for you. Just believe in his son, and all things will be possible. God is a spirit of positive energy he is all around you. The air you breath is a life he gave you. There is a place for all around Gods table. Just follow him and see. We are all blessed in some way or another. You may not know it but your parents has prayed for you. Your life has been covered with the blood of Jesus keeping the enemy away from you. Your ancestors has asked God to put a blessing on your family. When you keep this tradition of praying. Then pass it down to the next generation. God will keep his promise with you. No weapons formed against you shall prosper. When you are blessed you will find help for today, hope for tomorrow, and life for all eternity.

Head Shepherd
P.O.G
Loving Ministry

Spirit
BOLDNESS

When you are a believer you should be able to stand out from the world. People will feel your presence when you enter the room. The vibrations around you will be so strong. They will have no choice but to pay attention. They will hang on every word you say about God. Make statements of greatness, and empowerment. A spirit of excellence will always conquer evil have courage that no weapons formed against you shall ever prosper. Stand strong like a rock to defeat the evil ones plots. The most important things in life are not seeing but rather felt with our hearts. Deep inside we know what we are really made of, and we are indeed destined for greatness. It's the invisible inside world will that we've been programmed with thoughts, culture, and family, to have lost our power. Your thoughts create your life, your life doesn't create your thoughts. Thoughts and spirit, and energy, and everything are the creation of God. We can change our circumstances by changing our thought process. We have the power to change the face of our existence. Each of us do so by changing our thoughts. Change what you focus on and the world will change. Are you willing to change? Learn to love yourself and others never let No one tell you cannot do something, because with God all things become possible.

Head Shepherd
P.O.G.
Loving Ministry

Spirit
BUILT TO LAST!

Why is it when the difficulties of Life start setting in we are so quick to give up on life? You have an abundance of energy. All you have to do is tap into it your mind the power source. You just have to connect yourself to a higher frequency. Stop believing that there is limitations to your life. The universal God wants to lift you to the next dimension. There is no need to fear or have anxiety about anything. You are the ruler over your world just believe. There is a power in you beyond your imagination. And this 3d reality you have been program to think a certain way. You are more than a conqueror. We can achieve anything that we can perceive in our life. Raise your expectations, and start believing you can make all things possible. Stop letting man dictate to you how to live your life. He's only trying to turn us into Solomon and Gomorrah. He wants us to live in sin like he does. God has given you a spirit with a heart so that you can know the right things to do in life. This enemy has no control over you. We have the authority over him. We can make this world what we choose to when we believe. People of God we are all connected to one another. Let's stop letting the enemy divide us, and come together. To put back the positive energy in the world. When we believe on the same Accord. We can change the frequencies, and make this Society what it should be something of love. Take back your power, and start creating joy, peace for each other. We are the chosen ones of the light. Let the fear go, and be rulers of this world.

Head Shepherd
P.O.G
Loving Ministry

Spirit

CALL ON HIM!

P.O.G. do you know that your heavenly father wants a relationship with you? Call on him and ask that you want to get to know him. He's on call 24\7 waiting to hear from you. It don't have to be anything wrong for you to have to call on him. Just have a normal conversation with him. Like how you doing? My day is going well just talk. He is a really a good listener he won't interrupt you when you are speaking to him. God is a father with love in his heart for you. You don't have to go through anything in life alone. He will always be right by your side hand and hand guiding you through life problems. Take some time out and call on him, and see how happy you will be. There is nothing he won't forgive you of just ask him. If you want a real relationship with someone just ask him he is the one. The truth the light and the way. He will prepare a table before me in the presents of my enemies. You anointed my head with oil my cup runneth over surely, goodness and mercy, and love shall follow me all the days of my life. And through the length of my days the house of the lord shall be my dwelling place.

Head Shepherd
P.O.G.
Loving Ministry

CHANGE

....

Samuel 10:6 Then the spirit of the lord will rush upon you and you will prophesy with them. You will be changed into a different person.

Good morning people of God. There comes a time in everyone lives when you need to change the way you are living. Change is hard to do because we are set in our ways of doing things. Without change you will never know if things could have been different in your life. Change happen when you step out on faith and believe things will be better for you in life. Change must start in your mind first by thinking how you want things to be better. Better for you, and then take some action to make it better. Positive thoughts will always be good because they make you feel better and keep your spirits up. God knows what you need, and he will always guide you to what you are supposed to be in life. Change needs to happen in everyone's life just by putting God back in your life. With God there is nothing you cannot accomplish in life. Change will happen when your faith is strong and you truly believe in the father that all things are possible. Change is good when you are doing it to elevate the people in your life. Relationship, marriage, jobs, in health will all be better when you pray and ask god to help you. Don't be afraid of change when you have God on your side. Change your lifestyle and start living for others. And the things you seek in life will soon come your way. Change in longer – range matters whatever they may be is not easy. This is because people are mostly paying attention to what is imminent and pressing in their world. Compare all possible consequences of both your status quo and desired behaviors. If there are more positive results associated with the new behavior, your fears of the unknown are unwarranted.

Head Shepherd
P.O.G.

Spirit CALLING

Never try to fit in when you are designed to stand out. Everyone was designed with a specific gift to deliver to the world so remain to yourself be your individual unique self, and follow your purpose. We have a reason for being on this Earth. There is a power inside of you just learn how to tap into it. Believe in yourself knowing your capable of doing whatever you want in this life. If you feel dissatisfied with life, with your job, your ambition or any other feeling of dissatisfaction if life doesn't feel complete there is no sense of fulfillment you are always wanting for something to come along, and bring an amazing new change in your life all these may be pointing to a deeper longing as spiritual calling is when we realize that there is something missing something longing for fulfillment, and we just can't identify it or feel it. At some point we may discover that it is as easy as following our own heart, and that we meditate our conscious become clearer, and we are able to follow our heart. Don't believe if someone says it is this or that way. See what resonates for you try many things, and test them out. You will know when it feels right when the spiritual call comes answer it love, and peaceful thoughts will come into your life. Corinthians chapter 7 verse 12 nevertheless each person should have as a believer and whatever situation the Lord has assigned to them just as God has called them this is the rule I lay down in all the churches

Head Shepherd
P.O.G.
Loving Ministry

CELEBRATE

Exodus12:14 This is a day you are to commemorate, for the generations to come you should celebrate it as a festival to the lord.

G ood morning people of God. Its that time of year to celebrate being thankful and giving to families who are in need. Celebrations has been going on through out times. There are some misconceptions for some people to understand the reason for the celebrations. They choose to over drink or misuse drugs. Then they use this for a reason to do wrong to others. People in today's society is so scared to attend any kind of festivities or celebration. The fear of being harmed has stopped them from going to any social gatherings. The media has glamorized these chaotic events, and it has instilled fear into us. We are becoming a caged in society, so afraid of leaving our homes. It has gotten so bad that there is a service to bring you a big mac to your home. We don't go to the store anymore. You can get everything online. It is time to stop the madness, and start believing in your father again. He said no weapons formed against us shall prosper, and make your enemy your footstool. There is no need for fear or worry to be in your life, because you are on the side of the almighty Christ. There is nothing to fear but fear itself. So get out and live again. God wants us to be united as one people to grow his kingdom. So get out and spread the word that he is coming again. God loves a good celebration of songs, and dancing, and praising his name. Eat, drink, and be marry, because Gods coming again.

Head Shepherd
P.O.G.
Loving Ministry

Spirit

CALM

....

Proverbs 15:10 A quick- tempered person stirs up dissension, but one who is slow to anger calms a quarrel.

Good morning people of God. We as people of God must remain calm when life rages around us. Jesus can rebuke the storms of life if you just follow his words we must not let every little thing in life happen to us make us angry. The devil is working overtime to keep you upset the angrier you are the more control he has over you. Family and love ones are the first people he will work through to keep you angry. When you know the enemy how he works it will be less impossible to make you angry. We need to look at life with love in our heart first then go out in the world to try to show this to others. When you stay calm in troubled times things will always work out for you. Peace of mind is how Jesus was able to be killed on the cross; he knew his heavenly father was there with him. Calmness is something hard to do when the storm is raging all around you. Even soldiers in battle must keep their cool if they want to return to their love ones. If you just remain calm when all things around you are blowing up god promise to bring you through when you are calm you can see clearly what to do, and no harm will come to you. Peace is something the world needs, so all people of God can live together in harmony. Are you letting your impulse control you rather than taking a deep breath and saying Jesus Jesus to reflect on the best approach?

Head Shepherd
P.O.G.

Spirit
CHANGE

The Secret to change is to focus all of your energy not on fighting the old, but building the new. Education is the most powerful weapon which you can use to change the world. Clarify your your core values create a vision, believe that you can take on any challenges that comes your way in the pursuit of your happiness. Take personal responsibility. Let go of what you cannot control. Respond instead of reacting. Identify and understand what you want to change. Rid your life of negativity. Build a support network, and take baby Steps. These are some ways you can change your life. If you look around there is always someone in the world who grew up in a similar place, time, and situation, as you who manage to change their life for the better. In other words changing your life means making some tough decisions. So how badly do you want to change your life? And what are you willing to do, and to give up to make it happen? Once you decide to change your life come hail or high water. Suddenly almost anything is possible. It's not always that we need to do more, but rather that we need to focus on less. Do not look back on negative things in your life, you can't change the past but you can make your future. 2nd Corinthians chapter 5 verse 17 therefore if anyone is in Christ the new creation has come. The old has gone, the new is here!

Head Shepherd
P.O.G.
Loving Ministry

Spirit CHANGE

What would you attempt to do if you know you could not fail? Replace with something else especially something of the same kind that is newer or better. In order to make a difference in your life. You must change what you are doing to something that will benefit your life. It could be your job, friends, or your religion. The enemy has placed obstacles in your way. To stop you from God's glory. You can't change the direction of the wind, but you can adjust your sails to always reach your destination so, how do you start your new life today? It begins with repentance tell God you know you have sinned, and you want to turn away from your old ways of living. You must turn to Jesus, and ask him to come into your life. Once you do this God himself comes to live with in you by his spirit. Then you'll discover the same truth the apostle Paul discovered. " This means that anyone who belongs to Christ has become a new person. The old life is gone a new life has begun. We are surrounded by change, and it is the one thing that has the most dramatic impact on our lives. There is no avoiding it, because it will find you, challenge you, and force you to reconsider how you live your life. Spend some time trying to sort out what is important in your life, and why it is important. Then go in that direction let God guide you in life, and it will be what you want it to be.

Head Shepherd
P.O.G.
Loving Ministry

Spirit CHARACTER

Titus chapter 2:7-8 show yourself in all respects to be a model of good works, and in your teaching show integrity, dignity, and sound speech that cannot be condemned, so that and opponent may be put to shame, having nothing evil to say about us.

Your character is your personality especially how reliable and honest you are are. If someone of good character they are reliable and honest, God has given You traits of good value or good morals.. Good character is often something a person built over time. A moment when you have a difficulty to overcome can be a character building moment, because it helps you prove to yourself that you can make a good choice that is in the line with your values. The enemy don't want us to live a life of good morals. He has confused people to think bad is good, and good as bad the young have the future. The old have the past. But after all is said and done, the future will be, and the pass has been, someone's present. When you are young and have more future than the past. When you are old, you have more past than the future. So be someone of good character. By loving, caring, and sharing with someone.. Be proud of who you are, and not ashamed of how someone else sees you. If you love yourself, you do what's best for you. If you do what's best for you, you can give the best of yourself to those you love. It's going to be hard, but hard does not mean impossible!

Head Shepherd
P.O.G.
Loving Ministry

CHOICE

Job 22:25 There the almighty himself will be your gold, and the choicest silver for you.

Good morning people of God life are all about choices that does not mean that all choices are right, God has given us free will meaning that he leave it All up to us to make the right choice. I believe people want to do what is right in life, but Satan always makes them do wrong. It seems like the bad things in life are what is good. Satan has been playing tricks on us since the beginning of time. We all know what the bible tell us what is right and wrong. All things that feel good to you aren't always good for you. The bad places you hang out that was your choice. Why do we need to put our self in harm's way to have fun. Your mate in life was the one you choose to be with. You knew it was something wrong with them when you first meant them. People were telling you the bad things they were doing to others in life, but yet you still choose to be with them. We as P.O.G. must make the right choices. When God speaks to you just do what he ask of you. I believe if you choose to do well in life then your life will turn out good. We all know what is right and wrong our parents have taught us that. When you do good God will always bless you with good things. That is his laws and principles. When Satan starts to temp you to do bad just stop and pray. Tell God to take these thoughts away from you. God will always listen to you when you are doing the right things in life. Your first choice in the morning should be to thank God for waking you up this morning to see another wonderful day. People in life go around telling you how good they have it. You never see them at their worst. They are choosing to hide this away from you. People will never show you at first the real them. Because deep inside them there is no God. Without God inside of you life will never turn out for the good. Owning up to our choices ultimately makes us happier- because we can see that if we don't like our choices we have the power to change them. Choose God to guide your life, and let others see the God in you. We all have free will so use it to make the right choices in life.

Head Shepherd
P.O.G.
Loving Ministry

Spirit
CHARACTER

....

1 Corinthians 15:33 Do not be misled: "Bad company corrupts good character."

Have you ever heard the same clothes don't make the man. Why people spend so much money on their clothes, makeup, and shoes. Trying to be someone their not trying to impress others. It does not matter what's on the outside but what's on the inside is what counts. Your DNA is not like any other you have been made like God want you to be, unique in your ways. The character you should have is someone of substance. You have to feed your mind every day telling it you are great. Is not what happens but what you do that changes everything in your life. Its necessary you treat everyone right in with dignity in life. Be someone with character and compassion for others lead by example and let your words be able to teach others. Rely on yourself knowing that you must help others. Never complain never explain why you have to be a beacon of light. God has chosen you to get people through the tragedies of life. You have to realize all your struggles in life. When you help others it will be appreciated by Christ. Trusting yourself is the most important, when you're showing others the way to Christ. The most dangerous person is the one who listens, thinks, and observes. Do not allow people to dictate whats possible, stand firm in your faith in everything is possible. The way you view the world and every decision that you make in life. When the heart is pure that is when God resides inside of you. Be that person who change other lives.

Head Shepherd
P.O.G.
Loving Ministry

Spirit

CHARISMATIC

Everyone is great but most people won't do the hard work to show it! Greatness is inside everybody! Just get up and do what is difficult and embrace it. Exercising a compelling charm which inspires devotion and others. We have all seen the leader at the front of the room the one who holds an audience in a way bringing on laughter, and tears, and causing everyone to leave. Feeling challenged, inspired, and motivated. Though they may be experts in their field expertise alone doesn't explain the glowing responsibility they evoke in others. We as P.O.G. should want to make all people feel this way. So if you want people to feel welcome and a sense of belonging around you. Allow yourself to smile genuinely one of those really warm smiles that reach all the way up to the crinkles near your eyes. Yet positive and negative empathy is the ability to put yourself in someone else shoes and genuinely feel what they are feeling either good or bad. People who possess positive empathy don't get jealous. They get excited people who are generally enjoyable to be around are humble, and not arrogant. They don't wave awards in people's faces. They don't name drop for the sake of sounding important. They don't toot their own horns. They don't act like there above any person or situation. Let's be clear being vulnerable isn't easy. It's one of the most emotional challenging hurdles one can face overcoming the fear of being judged or criticized. Change your thoughts and you change your world.

Head Shepherd
P.O.G.
Loving Ministry

Spirit

COMFORT ZONE

Isaiah 49:13 Shout for joy, you heavens, rejoice, you earth burst into song, you mountains for the lord comforts his people and will have compassion on his afflicted ones.

Good morning people of God. We as P.O.G. say we believe in God. But we are so afraid to step out on faith to change our lives. We live in this comfort zone not willing to take any risk. Letting the enemy hold on to us not willing to break away from him. Having all these negative thoughts in our mind telling us we cannot do this. Stop living your live in a comfort zone get out and live your dream. God wants you to have your best life now. Start being daring and courageous again! Do the impossible being someone of excellence have high standards. Live life like you are always on an adventure to exotic places. Be grateful, and content to what God has given you already. He has so much more in store for your life. Be of good cheer have an attitude of happiness. Put God in charge of your life, and stop being so scared to take some risk. NO PAIN, NO GAIN! God will never lead you wrong believe in him, and yourself then life will be so comfortable.

Head Shepherd
P.O.G.
Loving Ministry

Spirit

COMPASSION

Sympathetic pity and concern for the sufferings of misfortunes of others. P.O.G. in order for us to change the world we must have compassion for one another. Stop living on selfish lives show concern for humanity! The challenges of life affect us all regardless of age, gender ethnicity, social status, or economic background. Each of us can you use assistance or words of encouragement during such trying times. Sometimes all people need is a little compassion, but not everyone knows how to show it. Displaying compassion can help improve the current mental or physical state feeling or situation of someone else. Offering a hug or word of encouragement in that moment of crisis can positively change the lives of those who feel vulnerable. To all the people out there don't ever let the worlds negativity disenchant you or your spirit. If you surround yourself with love then anything is possible. Its not happiness that makes you happy It's compassion for others that make you happy. You don't become what you want you, become what you believe. If you love yourself you do what's best for you. If you do what's best for you you can give the best of yourself to those you love. Lamentations 3: 22- 23 finally all of you be like minded Be like minded be sympathetic love one another be compassionate and humble.

Head Shepherd
P.O.G.
Loving Ministry

Spirit
COMPETENCE

....

Proverbs 3:21 My son, do not let wisdom and understanding out of your sight, preserve sound judgment and discretion.

The ability to do something successful or efficiently we all needed to learn how to be God-fearing people. Why are we so quick to let man tell us how to live our lives. Not once questioning his reason. The universal God only want us to have a glorious life. We all have a mountain we must climb in life. That is God getting us ready for problems in life. The climb is only making you stronger to deal with different scenarios in your life. Stay focus, and disciplined, God will get you to the top. Even though others may count you out stay consistent. We need all people to be a leader for God. Our children have been left to fend for themselves they need want and deserve someone to show them to Christ. It's time we all become leaders again. Teach the younger generation the meaning of the light. We have left it up to the enemy to show them it's time for us to take authority over their lives. Children are the future of the world We need to train them up well. Teach them things like honor respect and appreciation for one another. Show them unconditional love so they will know what it looks like. Let God guide us to be able to follow our hearts. We all need to come together to change the frequency of the world. When we are able to be one of the same level of positive that is when we can transform reality. Oh what a beautiful thing that would be to see imagine that.

Head Shepherd
P.O.G.
Loving Ministry

Spirit
COMPLAINING

Job 33:13 Why do you complain to him that he responds to no one's words?

Good morning people of God. People today always has something to complain about. They hate their job, their mate make them sick, their children don't listen to them. Not once trying to see the good things in life. If they was not complain g about something they will have nothing to say. Have you ever try seeing the positive in what you are complaining about. Like you have a job to go to, you have someone who loves you, God has blessed you with children. When you start seeing the good in things life will begin to change. Remember god left the people of Israel in the desert for forty years. Because they was complaining, and not listening to his words. Be grateful for what God has done for you already. He has giving you so much already, the air you breathe, and the sun that feeds your body vitamin d. Stop always wanting to talk about the bad things in life. Start speaking about what is good in the world today. Keep that mood level on high.

Head Shepherd
P.O.G.
Loving Ministry

Spirit
CHANGE YOUR FUTURE

Ecclesiastes 7:14 When times are good, be happy, but when times are bad, consider this: God has made the one as well as the other. Therefore, no one can discover anything about their future.

In order to change your future you must change how you look at yourself. When you look into the mirror what do you see? That person standing staring back at you how do you perceive them to be? You must envision someone of greatness, with limited possibilities. We all are builders you must know how to construct your life. Start by tearing down your old beliefs. A good home is built on a solid foundation. You must see the future that you want to build, and believe it with all your heart. The human spirit can get though anything. Stop letting fear hold you back from who you really are someone of greatness. Step out on faith, and believe you are unique In every way there is no turning back the future of your dream.

Take Accountability of your life. Speak words of encouragement over your life. Surround yourself with people who believe in your mission. Walk, talk, and act like you have already received this belief. It's time you must focus on the future you desire. Envision a world of abundance healing, and happiness, for everyone. Change how you think We can change the way we live. Let go of the pass loss and regrets just say no more! Freedom from a time clock to be your own boss. This world can be anything you want if you believe it could. Confront your fears, and stop running away from them. Give thanks for what God has done already in your life.

Head Shepherd
P.O.G.
Loving Ministry

Spirit
CONSISTENTLY

God says what a person consistently thinks that is what that person will become.

Good morning people of God. Whatever you want to accomplish in life you must start with a plan of action. You must believe and have faith in yourself and have the ability to achieve it. Your thought process must be on whatever you want to achieve in life every moment. Each and every day you must focus on this going forward in that direction towards your goal. Knowing god is there with you all the way. Pray every morning asking him to guide you there. You must keep heading in that direction no matter what. You will fail sometime in life but don't give up. Anything worth having in life is never easy. God didn't promise you that you will have an easy life. The storms will come but remember the morning will bring bright blue skies of calm. It is like learning to ride a bike. At first you fall then slowly you start to do better, and ride. Next thing you know you are popping wheelies. Life will always have obstacles in your way. Just learn how to get around them that's all. Don't let anything stand in your way of your dreams. Visualize greatness, holiness, and wellness. Just believe in these things and it shall come to pass. You're made in the image of almighty god! All things are possible through Christ! Change your thoughts and change your life into something incredible! Just believe in yourself, and have faith in God! The future belongs to those so prepare for it today.

Head Shepherd
P.O.G.
Loving Ministry

Spirit
CHEERFUL GIVER

2 Corinthians 9:7 each one of you should give just as he has decided in his heart, not reluctantly or under compulsion, because God loves a cheerful giver. Season's Greetings people of God.

It's that time of year again when we start thinking about the needs of others. God has promised that when you do well for others you will always have good things happen for you. Meaning be nice, appreciative when someone does good things for you. Just be grateful for what you already have in life. Then maybe God will reward you with more good things in life. Be a person of caring, sharing with others. The universe is set up like this. what you put out there it will come back to you. That is his law so be careful how you treat others because it will come back to you. You are always wondering why you don't have. It is because you don't give. Giving is the most wonderful thing you can do in life. It's better than playing the lottery. With giving you will always win. The part of happiness that we can control is about what we choose to focus on. We can constantly direct the way we focus our attention onto the good things in our life. This doesn't mean shedding out the negative. We cannot get rid of sad feelings, and negative thoughts, but we can acknowledge them. And then we can redirect focus back to what we have that makes us grateful. Research shows we can lean compactly to being grateful, and that doing so improves our health and relationships. So this holiday season be a grateful giver and not always wanting to be a receiver.

Head Shepherd
P.O.G.
Loving Ministry

Spirit CLARITY

....

John 8:43 Why is my language not clear to you? Because you are unable to hear what I say.

Good morning people of God. We as P.O.G. must be very clear on what we want to do with our lives. God has given us all a gift. You must find out what yours is. Just stop and look over your life and see what it is you're passionate about doing. Then start to build a plan of action, and write it down, and look at it each and every day. Let it be your road map as to where you want to go in life. A clear vision is needed at all times so that you can stay on the right path. There will be road blocks out there. But when you have God on your side he will lead you around them. Stay focus on improving your gift each and every day. Find a successful person with the same gift as you do. Then study them so you will know how to bring your gift to life. There will be people telling you that this won't happen for you. Don't loose faith just keep on believing in yourself? Nothing is easy in life if it's worth having. With discipline and perseverance you will be able to do all things in life. You must see it in order to believe it. Keep this vision in your mind at all times. Move toward it each and every day. Know that you are on the right track. Life will lead you there just keep believing in your dream. Remember the importance of every time you say" I don't know" to just slow down, and focus on your breath and look at your emotions after you say " I don't know" and just see, is there a feeling that comes up. Even if it's just a little glimpse of a feeling, try to amplify that experience because the desperate search for clarification and answers can be a ruse by your mind to impress or suppress an emotional experience. Many times the reason you're trying to suppress it is because it's not something that you're very comfortable with. So if you're not comfortable with being afraid, it might be fear: if you don't like to be sad, it could be that. The question may not be as important as you think it is. It may just be strategy to keep your mind turning so you can't feel what really needs to be felt and dealt with.

Head Shepherd
P.O.G.
Loving Ministry

Spirit
COMMITMENT

....

1 Kings 8:61 And may your heart be fully committed to the Lord our God, to live by his decrees and obey his commands, as at this time.

Good morning people of God. People in the world today cannot commit to anything long term. We are so quick to lose interest in anything that takes time. Always wanted the here and now in life. To be a person of true commitment you must be able to go the long hall. Not giving up when things start being difficult. The hard times in life is when, God is shaping you so that you can be strong. The devil knows that most folks cannot endure to the end. He will make you think to give up on your dreams and just go back to being status quo. Any amount of discomfort we quickly throw in the towel on life. When you start out on your journey in life you should want to finish it till the end. Let's stop being people who aren't willing to go through some pain, and suffering in life. God did not promise us a comfortable life. Your mind has control over your emotions. You can change anything with the right thoughts. Be committed to see it through no matter what. Finish what you start and cross the finish line and be a winner. Difficulties is something we all must go through. You must know how to pass the test. God says just ask and he will give you the answers. Be that person who is committed in life. No matter what situation you are going through you should have some kind of commitment to see it through family, and friends, love ones and career stand strong believing this is what a life of commitment is all about.

Head Shepherd
P.O.G.
Loving Ministry

Spirit
CREATION

Psalm 96:13 Let all creation rejoice before the lord, for he comes, he comes to judge the earth. He will judge the world in righteousness, and the people in his faithfulness.

Good morning people of God. If I were to ask you who you are, would you know without a shadow of a doubt who you were? People spend so much time trying to be someone who God did not create them to be. Every person on earth has a purpose in life. God has given you a talent to use to help others. That gift is who God want you to be. We all know what we like doing in life, its just we are afraid to step out in faith. If you want to be who God created, you to be you must believe in yourself. Knowing God is there with you all the way. Have courage to go after your dreams and make it a reality. Dream big there is nothing impossible when God is on your side. He wants you to be who he created you to be someone of importance. Life will never be like what you wanted to be. If you don't believe in the father. Stop being afraid who God created you to be. You're made in the image of the almighty God. There are great powers in you just open up your mind, and envision great things for yourself. People will never understand why you are different. But know they can see the changes in you. Don't let them talk you out of your destiny. Stay focus until you have achieved your dreams. When you do this all things are possible with Christ.

Head Shepherd
P.O.G.
Loving Ministry

Spirit

CONFIDENCE

It's all about who we are inside it is all about what we are willing to give to get what we want. I don't believe you have to be better than everybody else. I believe you have to be better than you ever thought you could be. The feeling or belief that one can rely on someone or something for something firm trust.. Trust God and you will never be led wrong believe in your ability to accomplish what you want in life. Be bold, courageous, and achieve all the things which are good. Walk in faith like you know this will happen for you in life. Don't let any negative thoughts enter your mind. When you feel not good enough, or not strong enough remember who God says you are! Isaiah 32:17 the fruit of the righteous will be peace is effect will be quietness and confidence forever. Your own beliefs are the most powerful forces that influence your existence. They are determined what you are what you perceive, and How you perceive it. They influence your thoughts your expectations, and your actions. They shape your personality.. They even affect the outcome of your actions, and the way others perceive and respond to you. Does it sometimes seem like everyone around you is confident, and sure of themselves? Chances are they have doubts just like you. So what's The Secret they've discovered about how to be confident? They know that confidence is not something you have. It's something you create. Being confident is nothing more than a belief in yourself. It's the feeling of certainty that you can accomplish whatever you set your mind to.

Head Shepherd
P.O.G.
Loving Ministry

Spirit
CONSCIOUSNESS

Hebrews 10:2 Otherwise, would they not have stopped being offered? For the worshipers would have been cleansed once for all, and would no longer have felt guilty for their sins.

Do you know you have two conscious your subconscious and your mind. Your conscious mind can only see this 3-D Five sense reality. The subconscious is where your power lives. In there you are able to manifest how you want to live your life. You have to use your imagination, and see yourself doing the impossible. Even when you're asleep at night visualize how you would like your reality. Dream amazing things, and be creative of the outcome. We must learn how to reprogram the subconscious from the old ways of Thinking. You have been taught that you are a common person but in reality you are amazing. We are living in the end times of this evil having authority over us. We must tell our self conscious no weapon formed against us will ever prosper. I am a victor and not the victim. The 6000 years for the evil one ruling over this Earth has ended. We are moving into the Golden Age where there will be peace, love, happiness, and prosperity, for all. Recondition yourself seeing life like it should be filled with positivity. Let's be Warriors of the light, And not let this enemy have control over life. He's only able to do what you give him consent to do take back your power. Follow your heart start loving sharing, and caring, for each other we must learn to govern our selves and stop letting men have that authority. When we are able to stand as one by filling this universe with positive energy. Then it will be Heaven on Earth. We are all connected we are the body of Christ. Where we go as one, we all go.

Head Shepherd
P.O.G.
Loving Ministry

Spirit CONNECTED

If you're going to do anything Do it to be it! P.O.G. we need to be one big ball of energy connected to 1. Whenever we around the same frequency. We can change the channel of the world. Each day in every part of the world. We all become closer and closer to one another. Technology empowers us to do great things together but technology is but 1 mechanism through which we connect. Let us. Not forget the human connection we experience every day through family, community, and personal and professional networks. Our connections is a gift. So take that phone, computer, brand network platform or whatever resources are at your disposal, and act. Being better connected is not an end itself is a great new beginning filled with possibility. Loneliness occurs when there is a lack of genuine human connection to other people. Let's consider the human connection definition. Why the power of human connection is important to our lives, and how to build meaningful relationship With others. Human connection is a deep bond that's form between people when seen and value. During an authentic human connection, people exchange positive energy with one another, and build trust human connection makes you feel heard, and understood and give you a sense of belonging. Human beings are social species wired to connect with all humanity and gentleness, with patience, bearing with one another in love eager to maintain the unity of the spirit, and the bond of peace.

Head Shepherd
P.O.G.
Loving Ministry

CONSENT

Philemon 1:14 But I did not want to do anything without your consent, so that any favor you do would not seem forced but would be voluntary.

Throughout time people have always look to others to guide them in life. Even though the outcome may not be what they like. They still give others control of their life. Your heavenly father has provided you with principles that you shall live by. We all know what is the right thing to do in life. But at the same time we let the world tell us how to live our lives. We are always trying to be politically correct worrying about what others will think of us. There comes a time where you should speak out, and when you see something that isn't right. Christ was crucified so that you may have these freedoms to speak out when you see evil. Stop being afraid of what others will think about you. God has prepared you to be someone of Hope to show others to the path of righteousness. We must stop submitting to this evil. Letting him turn this world into Solomon and Gomorrah. God has given you eyes, ears, and a heart to know when something isn't right. When you are able to speak with words of conviction. That is your power that is within you. When you give God authority over your life. There is nothing the enemy can do to you. Start being that Warrior for Christ, and make this world a place where your children, and their children can live a life of freedom, and prosperity. Love & Faith is something we must all have if we want to make this into reality. We all have been brainwashed by human. It's time to wake up, and realize who the real Sin savior is the one with the truth the light and the way.

Head Shepherd
P.O.G.
Loving Ministry

Spirit
CONSEQUENCES

Ezekiel 16:58 You will bear the consequence of your lewdness, and your detestable practices declares the lord.

Good morning people of God. P.O.G. you need to know that there are consequences when you don't follow Gods laws. We think we can do whatever we want to do in life. But remember there is always a price you must pay when you are doing wrong. Your father would never let you get away with doing wrong with out disciplining you may not know when it will come but it will happen to you. The bad breaks, sickness, lost of job, these are some of the ways you will be punished for doing something wrong. God knows whats in your heart and mind so be a person with integrity. You may think you have gotten away with something but in the end you will be judged for doing wrong. The enemy is so busy filling our heads with bad things just look around you its everywhere. Its so easy to do wrong its like second nature. Why is that? God has given you free will over your life. He trust you to do what is right. Our spiritual faith is so weak compared to the Devil temptations. Your heavenly father does not like to punished you. Remember spare the rod spoil the child. Your father wants you to stop doing wrong in life. Do the right thing just ask him to help you. Prayer is the way to a better life. See yourself being a better person then your mind will conceive it. God will always help you through life difficulties. Believe this he will always be there for you. The devil has so many tools for you to do wrong in life. Stay focus on God then life will be more happy and rewarding. You have a power in you to make that change. So do it.

Head Shepherd
P.O.G.
Loving Ministry

Spirit

CONTROL YOUR MIND!

Master your emotions, master your thoughts, focus always on with you want in life. It's just as easy to focus on what you want as what you don't want, but what you want will bring you much more joy. Control demands, commitment and commitment demands effective time management. Don't waste precious moments! Your goals deserve undivided attention. Use your Mind wisely. In our life we face many difficulties and failures no matter how hard we try to get things better. Stay in control of your mind, and keep your emotions positive. We often have so many thoughts a day that its hard to feel like we're in complete control. Sometimes it feels like they overrun your brain. That's when you know that you need to learn how to control your mind. You can learn how to swap those unwanted negative thoughts for more positive thinking. It won't happen with the snap of your fingers, but with sustained effort, you'll be able to focus your thoughts on more productive, positive things. We know that positive thinking and optimism can actually improve our health and physical well being. But unwanted thoughts can fill us with negative emotions, and make us feel defeated. They take us away from the present moment by having us dwell on the past or feel anxious about the future. Having control over our mind helps us achieve our short-term and long-term goals. It helps us get through our days professionally and personally with a clear, confident growth mindset.

Head Shepherd
P.O.G.
Loving Ministry

Spirit
COURAGE

Spiritual courage fortifies us as we ask questions about purpose, and meaning of course many people find the foundation of this courage in an organization religion, but there are also other ways to develop spiritual courage. Spiritual courage means being available to the deepest questions about why we are here, what is my life for, do I have a purpose? Spiritual courage allows us to encounter people of different religious, faiths, and spiritual traditions, without judgment. Don't be afraid to do things outside the norm. People may criticize you but guess what? For every one person that is negative there are 100 other people who are for you. Focus on the positive, and drown out the negative. Our greatest fear is not that we are inadequate, but that we are powerful beyond measure! Believe in yourself. You are braver than you think, and more talented than you know, and capable of more than you can imagine keep putting in the work! We often let fear dictate our decision. However living a courageous life is one of the ways to find success in business and in life. Courage is the first of human virtues, because it makes all other possible. Do the thing that you fear as the quickest way to conquer fear if you feel afraid of other people seeing who you are open up and become more valuable 1Corinthians 16:13 Be on guard stand firm in the faith. Be courageous be strong.

Head Shepherd
P.O.G.
Loving Ministry

Spirit
COURAGE

....

Oftentimes the real challenge is overcoming ourselves. We have to see ourselves in a new way, and have a vision for what the best version of ourselves look like. Being more courageous in your life will help you respond appropriately to risk an accomplished positive things in your life. But it takes work to move beyond your fears in fact being courageous is about thinking things through, examining the risk, and rewards and acting in spite of the fear that inevitably sets in. Yes If you have been struggling with fear, and want to feel more courageous in your life there are a number of ways you can exercise your courage muscles, and make the most out of every situation. Instead of assuming that being fearful is a bad thing look at it as an opportunity to learn more about who you are, and why you might be afraid, or less than thrilled about stepping out of your comfort zone. You might find that if you take the time to name your fear, and understand why it's there that you will uncover a better idea of how to overcome it, or be courageous in spite of it. When it comes to living a life filled with courage it helps to begin by identifying what you're good at as well as where you have been successful. Deuteronomy chapter 31 verse 6 be strong and courageous do not be afraid or terrified because of them, for the Lord your God goes with you, he will never leave you or forsake you

Head Shepherd
P.O.G
Loving Ministry

Spirit
CREATE

Psalms 51:10 Create in me a pure heart, O God, and renew a steadfast spirit within me.

People of God we all was created in the image of God. We are able to create whatever environment that we choose to exist in. We have been given dominion over this world to create something beautiful. When you're able to believe that is when you are tapping into who you really are in life. You have the answer to all mysteries in life. You must anticipate that God will guide you in life. You must believe that you will choose the right spiritual path in life. This is not where God wants you to be, moved forward with your life. Create whatever reality you want for your life, call on the warrior spirit inside of you, and Be who God created you to be! You must have faith you must believe in yourself. Self confidence come from when you believe you can achieve. There are no limits in what you can build out of your life. Never lose sight on your goals in life. Use your imagination, or ideas to create the world you choose. This universe is filled with possibilities. You Just have to decide which one you want to achieve in life. God has given you a unique opportunity to build whatever environment that you can be productive. We just have to let go of our ego, and know the heavily father will never fail us. Focus on the world you want to create, and you will manifested! Raise your vibration, and thoughts and then this will happen for you. Trust your intuition that is God talking to you. It is never too late to be who you might have been.

Head Shepherd
P.O.G.
Loving Ministry

Spirit
CREATIVITY

....

Just because your parents live in a small town got married early, and worked a 9 to 5 for 30 years, that doesn't mean you have to do the same. You have choices and with growth of the Web your choices have compounded expeditiously. You control your life and what happens in it, and once you realize that fully you Give yourself room to grow, experiment, and begin designing the life of your dreams. The 1st step towards Designing your ideal life is to realistically assess yourself, and figure out where you are now. As much as we may think that we can easily handle a new challenge with our past experiences people find themselves getting scared when they feel unfamiliar with their future, because they're afraid. They'll fail or make mistakes. We become familiar with certain things, but not others. But thinking about those things that you want to do or would like to accomplish helps you get more confident in facing challenges. Remember the difference between ordinary and extraordinary. Successful people do what unsuccessful people are not willing to do. Don't wish it were easier wish you We're better. We were put here on this Earth to beautify the world. So step Into your power and start creating a reality of love. Ask God how can I be of service in this world, and be able to serve others as well. Controlling our minds is a great thing not to move along with our circumstances, our distraction Just move ahead of them.

Head Shepherd
P.O.G.
Loving Ministry

Spirit

CONTENTMENT

....

Philippians 4:12 I have experienced times of need and times of abundance. In any and every circumstance I have learned the secret of contentment, whether I go satisfied or hungry have plenty or nothing.

People of God we must be more content for what we have in life. It don't matter how old you are just be content for what God has given you. Not everyone can be big baller shot callers. Know that if you want more out of life you need to ask for it, and follow his laws. You need action with your faith in order for things to happen for you. Whatever you want in life it all starts in your mind first. You must believe to achieve. Look at yourself of a child of the most high; you're made in an image of the almighty God. You that same power in you to make whatever you want in life to happen for you. Just as long as god is in it. Stop seeing yourself as a nobody and start seeing yourself as a somebody. In whatever you are doing in life. Be content with what you have. God will always give you more if you believe in his son. You may not be rich in material things but be rich in your personality. Be happy, joyful then others will want to be around you and do things to help you. The core business of life is to make sure the way you experience the world matches up to the way we want to experience it. Making things be the way we want them to be is what we do all day. But God may have a different purpose for our life. If things are not working out for you in life, ask God for some guidance. Start looking at life differently when perspective suddenly shifts. A new point of view sweeps away the familiar ways of looking at things. Once seen with fresh eyes, a new perspective cannot be undone. Let the Lord guide you through life.

Head Shepherd
POG

Spirit
CORDIAL

2 Samuel 2:6 now may the Lord show you true kindness. I also will reward you, because you have done this deed.

Good morning people of God. People of God love to hear people say nice things about them. Like Happy birthday, congratulations and good job. We all need that to help make us happy on the inside knowing someone care about our well being. When you put out words of kindness it will always come back to you like a boomerang. There isn't a person on earth who doesn't like to be told something good about them. We as people of God should always be on the look out to say something good about some one. God has promise when you do well to others he would do well for your life. A word of kindness goes along way even people talk to their plants so they can be healthy and strong. Your children should be told great job when they bring home good grades. Words filled with positivity will always work out for the good. When someone is feeling good about themselves it makes them want to do for others. This is his plan for us to love and help others in society. Letting someone know you care about their well being makes you a person of God. If you are kind to others it generates a circle of positivity which will increase compassion for others and yourself. Kindness is a simple act of being friendly to someone we meet. There are some people in the world that I find it hard to be kind to., but I've come to realize that when I direct hate at them, I'm the one who suffers .Because God says be kind to one another and show love like Jesus did for you to save your soul from hell.

Head Shepherd
P.O.G.

Spirit
DARING

Proverbs 21:29 The wicked put up a bold front, but the upright give thoughts to their ways.

A person of action adventurous and audaciously bold. Don't let the enemy keep you in fear from being able to take on a life. God did not give you a spirit of fear. Know yourself and don't be afraid of the challenges of life. It's time to stop looking for what you don't have, and put your full attention on what you do have. It's time to bring out the best version of yourself so that everyone around you will notice. Be grateful for what you already have while you find yourself. If you aren't grateful for what you already have what makes you think you would be happy with more? The happiness of your life depends upon the quality of your thoughts therefore guard them and take care that you don't entertain any negative ones. No matter if you are shy or already outgoing any person may want to be more of an extrovert. This type of person is generally outgoing, energetic, and likely to say yes to adventure or excitement. It may be difficult to overcome social anxieties, and walk up to someone, But this is one of the best ways not only to be more outgoing, but also more approachable. If you show courage people will open up to you. Don't be afraid to go where no one has gone before. God will always protect you when you're loving towards others the stronger your mindset is the greater your skill set is going to be! What you believe is what becomes real.

Head Shepherd
P.O.G.
Loving Ministry

Spirit
DARKNESS

Psalms 84:11 For the Lord God is a sun and a shield, The Lord will give grace and glory, no good thing will be with held from them that walk uprightly.

Good morning people of God. In the beginning the earth was dark and void. God created angels before man, and put them here on earth. He wanted them to beautify, and glorify the earth. But Lucifer talk some angels to turn away from God. Then the earth was left with darkness, and decay. Then God made man to do the same to beautify, and glorify the earth. But instead of doing this man decided to live in darkness in their evil ways. They tried to hide in the dark from the light so no one would know about their sins. The priest in catholic churches are molesting kids, and it is kept quiet. People are keeping their drug addiction in the dark so no one will know about it. In some marriages there is some adultery that is being kept in the dark. Men believe if they keep it in the dark that no one will find out about it. The devil has twisted our minds to believe that this is true. I'm here to tell you! God knows whats in your heart and mind. We must come out of the darkness, and live in the light. Stop manipulating people about making them believe we are living right. In the light everyone can see you are living right. Step into the light of righteousness, and be a person of excellence. In the light there is nourishment so your body can grow with vitamin d to make your bodies healthy, and strong. God lives in the light he is that positive energy you feel when things are going right. In the light you can see clear nothing can be hidden from you. That is why the enemy like the darkness so much. God created you to live in the light, and make this world a beautiful place. Remember only love can drive out all the darkness.

Head Shepherd
P.O.G.
Loving Ministry

Spirit
DECEITFULNESS

Matthew 13:22 And the one on whom seed was sown among the thorns, this is the men who hears the word, and worry of the world and the deceitfulness of wealth choke the word, and it becomes unfruitful.

Good morning people of God! Dishonesty is a quality which sits at conflicting ends with truth. Many of us have probably experienced dishonest people at some point in our lives. You will typically find that they are because of a desire for acceptance, love or to address a personal need, rather than because of ill desires. We as people live our lives and in its masquerade not knowing who we are less on others knowing who we are. We teach our kids to be something that they don't understand at an early age in life. Boys are trying to tell the girls what they want to hear, not meaning any of the words they say, just after one thing, and that is a conquest. Girls are told by their mother to look for the boy with the deep pockets to buy them things that they like even though there are no feelings for the boy, but will do what they need to do to get him to buy them something. We try to keep up with the Jones's always trying to have something even though we might not need it. When the bill collector calls, you tell them the untruth about why you can't pay your bill. We are in a relationship with someone not knowing each other at all and afraid to show the REAL us. From the beginning we are trying to be a person who we thought the other person would like us to be, not letting them know the real us. Now, we are married with children and still the games continue. Soon we start sneaking around with someone else who can take care of our needs, the one thing we cannot tell our mate about. Next thing you know we are in divorce court, still not able to tell the truth to your mate. Why do we spend life trying to be someone we are not, thinking society will accept someone better than who you really are. Jesus said, "Tell the truth, and the truth shall set you free, from worried about being caught up." It is so bad that other cultures are even trying to be like American people and not following their own customs anymore. When will people be what God created them to be in life? Honesty is the best policy. Remember, you would rather be slapped by the truth than kissed by a lie.

Head Shepherd
POG
Loving Ministry

Spirit
DEAF EAR

James 1:19 Understand this, my dear brothers and sisters! Let every person be quick to listen, slow to speak, slow to anger. Good morning People of God.

This world is filled with all kinds of crazy things that will affect us all. There are historic earthquakes, hurricanes, and floods, but yet we seem not to care about. Countries are trying to go to war with one another by testing there nuclear bombs. People are hating and fighting and killing one another just because. It seems we are not noticing the sign of the time. Even when day turn suddenly tonight. The bible has foretold these things. Even the man with the bible in his hand is not being listened too, it falls on deaf ears. We as POG must stop and listen and start telling people about these things. So that they can prepare their family and friends for them. We must come together and be as one. The enemy is hard at work trying to destroy this world. There must be more compassion between each other. The time has come are you ready to do God's will? Because our will is not making things better here on earth. POG has to come together and have a voice of reason. Letting others know that God is the only way to salvation. Time has come to stop the hating of people, and start caring, and sharing again. The signs are all around us you just have to open your eyes, ears, and heart. God is telling you the time is near for the battle with the evil one. We must prepare now join together meaning all POG must stand as one. We all know what is right from wrong. Just be good to one another. Love as Jesus did when he was here on earth. The heavenly father knows what's in your heart. Love yourself then it will be easy to love others. The devil has taken so much from us. It's time to take it back. Let's be ready, and listen to the man with the bible in his hand. No weapon that is formed against thee shall prosper, and every tongue that shall rise against thee in judgment thou shalt condemn. This is the heritage of the servants of the Lord, and their righteousness is of me saith the Lord.

Head Shepherd
P.O.G
Loving Ministry

Spirit
DECISION

Psalm 17:2 make a just decision on my behalf! Decide what is right!

Good morning people of God. We have the power to decide what road we like to go down in life. Whatever you want to do in life it is all up to you to do. You are the GPS of your destination in life. Good or bad God has left the choice for you to make. Whatever you want to be or do in life you must think about it first. Start with an idea of it, and then write it down on paper. Then this will be your road map to where you want to go in life. God said you must believe before you can receive anything in life. Your mind has two sides of thoughts positive or negative. Whatever a person think that Is what they will be, so think about greatness. Program and train your mind to think positive all the time. This will be difficult, but it is a must if you want good things in life. Stay on a path of righteousness do for others, and love yourself as well as others. Let your character be of God like be an example for others. We make so many quick decisions unconsciously, others we agonize over. We choose action and form opinions, via mental processes which are influence by biases reasons, emotions, and memories. Some questions whether we even have free will. Others believe it is well within our power to make choices that will lead to better well –being. The biggest decision that you have to make in life is do you believe. Because when you believe all the doors of life will be open for you. There will be no more mystery about life just a clear vision of life. Make the decision to believe something greater than men.

Head Shepherd
P.O.G.
Loving Ministry

Spirit

DO YOU HAVE FAITH IN PEOPLE OR GOD?

2 Samuel you prove to be loyal to one who is faithful: you prove to be trustworthy to one who is innocent.

Good morning people of God. We as people of God always want other peoples to figure out our problems in life. Taking their advice without any thought of it being right. Waiting on the hook up from people to help us with our career and financial woes. Telling them our life problems not once thinking about has the person been through what we are going through right now. If someone has not been through what you are going through how can they help you with a solution? The Bible says you don't know what a person is going through unless you have walked in their shoes. So why we put so much faith in people to help us and not in the almighty God? When the storms of life come your way I mean an f 5 storm just tearing everything apart. Look around you and see all the people you put faith in are gone taking cover. There is one who is still there with you keeping you safe from harm that is God. He will never abandon you in any situation in life. Just have faith and believe in Jesus. There will always be more sunny days and fewer storms remember put your trust in God and not man.

Head Shepherd
P.O.G.

Spirit

DEEP BREATH

Job 12:10 In whose hand is the life of every creature and the breath of all the human race.

Good morning people of God. We as people of God need a moment of quiet and calm. Before the stresses of the day overtake us. Just pray to yourself this is going to be a blessed day over and over. Sitting in a quiet place when the rush of the day start like you are going through a drive through, and they messed up your order take a deep breath. When you are in traffic and someone cut you off take a deep breath. The boss start yelling at you about being late take a deep breath. Tell yourself God is in control and keep moving on. Being upset and angry all day long is not good for you, or the people around you. When the children are not trying to hear you. Just take a deep breath and breathe There are times in life when things are chaotic the trick is you must remain in control by keeping calm. When the storms of life come your way breathe deep, and just ride them out. God is right there by your side holding your hand. When everything start going wrong in life you must keep a positive outlook of life. Know in your mind that it will turn out for the good of it. God has promised you he will let no harm come to you. Believe he is your heavenly father and is watching out for you. Keep calm when things start going wrong in life. Your joy is worth a lot more than you can imagine. The devil does not want you to be happy. Take a deep breath and say devil loose me. I know life can be hard sometime that you can't breathe. God did not promise you life would be easy. Just hold on change is coming. Have positive thoughts believing in the good things in life. Breathe deep and say god is good nothing will take my joy away from me. God calls us as individuals and as P.O.G. to fight evil, poverty, injustice, disease, and prejudice. Spiritual eyes are open as we reveal Gods love and mercy through our actions. You must believe to receive!

Head Shepherd
P.O.G.
Loving Ministry

Spirit
DECISIONS

In order to change your life. You must make a decision to do so. life is full of decisions you have to make. The only way to change your life is making a decision knowing how to make good decisions like what to wear to a job interview, or how to invest your money. Could be the key to living your best life, and being able to make these decisions in a timely manner, and feeling confident about your decision making skills could save you a lot of time and hassle. When you make better decisions it also means you're learning from your mistakes, and learning from your mistakes is a crucial aspect of personal development. You cannot lead without being able to make good decisions. Philippines 4:6-7 Do not be anxious about anything but in everything by prayer, and supplication with Thanksgiving let your request be made known to God. And the peace of God which surpasses all understanding will guard your heart and your mind in Christ Jesus, don't limit yourself. Many people limit themselves to what they think they can do. You can go as far as your mind lets you. What you believe remember you can achieve. The secret to change is to focus all your energy not on fighting the old but building the new. The difference between average people, and achieving people is their perception of their response to failure. You can sit and talk about what you are going to do. But until you actually do what you say is when you will experience success!

Head Shepherd
P.O.G.
Loving Ministry

Spirit
DEVOTION

Love, loyalty, or enthusiasm, for person activity or cause climb the mountain so you can see the world not so the world can see you. Continue to grow, move, and create again. Don't let unfortunate things stop you from building yourself up. But rather use it as a stepping stone to level up. What is your greatest desire? We often read today's passage, and assume that it means. God will give us whatever we want. It's not uncommon for someone to talk about a prayer request, and then add. God promise to give me the desire of my heart. But in context that scripture reveals that god's principle for purifying our desire, and issue a call. For devotion to God. To delight in God means to take pleasure in discovering more about God and in following God. As we do the Holy Spirit of lying's our hearts desires with God which position us to experience god's blessings. We may not always be able to control what happens to us but. We can control how we react to it. There is always an opportunity to be stronger, and grow wiser for those who are suffering from anxiety and depression. May we all accept God and surrender our worries, and our problems to God. You are not alone. God is always with you. God will never put us in the situation that we can't overcome. Let's trust God's plan. Surrender everything to God, and God will always be there for you. This is a sign of you to strengthen your faith, and God. Except God into your life

Head Shepherd
P.O.G.
Loving Ministry

Spirit

DECEITFULNESS

Matthew 13:22 And the one on whom seed was sown among the thorns, this is the men who hears the word, and worry of the world and the deceitfulness of wealth choke the word, and it becomes unfruitful.

Good morning people of God! Dishonesty is a quality which sits at conflicting ends with truth. Many of us have probably experienced dishonest people at some point in our lives.

You will typically find that they are because of a desire for acceptance, love or to address a personal need, rather than because of ill desires.

We as people live our lives and in its masquerade not knowing who we are less on others knowing who we are. We teach our kids to be something that they don't understand at an early age in life. Boys are trying to tell the girls what they want to hear, not meaning any of the words they say, just after one thing, and that is a conquest. Girls are told by their mother to look for the boy with the deep pockets to buy them things that they like even though there are no feelings for the boy, but will do what they need to do to get him to buy them something.

We try to keep up with the Jones's always trying to have something even though we might not need it. When the bill collector calls, you tell them the untruth about why you can't pay your bill. We are in a relationship with someone not knowing each other at all and afraid to show the REAL us. From the beginning we are trying to be a person who we thought the other person would like us to be, not letting them know the real us. Now, we are married with children and still the games continue. Soon we start sneaking around with someone else who can take care of our needs, the one thing we cannot tell our mate about. Next thing you know we are in divorce court, still not able to tell the truth to your mate. Why do we spend life trying to be someone we are not, thinking society will accept someone better than who you really are. Jesus said, "Tell the truth, and the truth shall set you free, from worried about being caught up." It is so bad that other cultures are even trying to be like American people and not following their own customs anymore. When will people be what God created them to be in life? Honesty is the best policy. Remember, you would rather be slapped by the truth than kissed by a lie.

Head Shepherd
POG
Loving Ministry

Spirit DIFFERENT

....

Romans 12:6 We have different gifts, according to the grace given to each of us. If your gift is prophesying, then prophesy in accordance with your faith.

Good morning people of God. Why is it that everybody wants to be like who they see on social media. A movie star, the rock star, and athletes why we just can't be people with characteristics? It has gotten so bad that other cultures have given up their customs to be like Americans. America has enslaved its people, dropped atomic bombs on other countries, and went to war to take their wealth. We are a great nation, but the enemy has confused us to believe doing wrong is the right thing to do. Every country wants to be a super power. To rule over others and take their dignity. Our heavenly father created us to use the most powerful weapon in the universe, and that is love. But yet we let the enemy keep, our mind twisted thinking hating each other is what we are supposed to do. Even from the early biblical days every destruction,and war has been between people not understanding each other. The time has come to make a difference to stop the violence, and corruption in this world. We must learn to love one another again. Put God back into our lives, and stop letting the world show us how to live. Whatever you want in life you must have love in your heart. Then your father will happily bring it to pass for you. Lets be people with dignity, and respect for one another. Don't be like the world. Try to make a difference in this world with goodness, and grace.

Head Shepherd
P.O.G.
Loving Ministry

Spirit
DIRECTION

If you don't know where you are going. How will you know when you get there? We the P.O.G. needs to start taking direction from the universal God. Let the spirit lead you to becoming a better person. When you are able to stop listening to your ego that is when you are listening to God. God is always there for us. We just need to listen when the spirit is talking to you. Following direction is an important life skill, and one that is especially hard for some people. Attention deficit disorder don't tune out now if you don't think you have it. Giving direction to people is about more than telling them what to do. Good direction for people help them learn about their world, what is right and what is wrong, and what kind of behavior you expect. People need consistency, and structure to thrive. Finding the right direction in life is an existential problem we all face. A direction in life means getting goals for yourself to be successful. With out goals, there will be no motivation, and with no motivation you can't move forward in life. Whether your in your 30's fresh out of school or just retired trying to figure out your new direction, in life can be tough. This is also relevant if you are living a life your not satisfied with, and hope to change your life's direction. Finding the right direction in life is not something that happens to you its something you create this means that at some point, you have to stop thinking about taking action and start acting. Nothing is impossible. The word itself says I'm possible! There is only one corner of the universe you can be certain of improving and that's your own self.

Head Shepherd
P.O.G.
Loving Ministry

Spirit
DISCIPLINE

The power to do great things Does it come from nowhere? It comes from within you. If you're committed to doing something you'll find the strength to see it through. So whatever it is that you want to achieve go out and do it. You either make moves or make excuses. Set goals or smash them you can come up with excuses, but the bottom line is no one can stop you but you. Learning to effectively lead yourself, and others all come down to discipline. Happiness success, and fulfillment, stem from focus and self control. It may be hard to believe when you're facing, and all you can eat buffet the prospect of making a quick buck or the lazy lure of sleeping in versus getting on the platform, but studies show that people with self discipline are happier. Because with discipline and self control we actually accomplish more of the goals we truly care about. Self discipline is the bridge between goals defined, and goals accomplished. Your brain doesn't Differentiate between real, and imaginary memories. So when you imagine something Vividly your brain chemistry change As if you've actually experienced it. Self discipline is a practice you will not be perfect every day. Whats important is showing up each day ready to try. So what changes are you going to make today? Be consistent. Consistency is key when it comes to building discipline try to follow through on your task and goals on a daily basis even if you don't like it. Nobody's going to be as dedicated to it as you are!

Head Shepherd
P.O.G.
Loving Ministry

Spirit
DIVISION

Mark3:25 If a house is **divided** against itself, that house cannot stand. Good morning people of God.

We are families that are coming a part at the seems. We are a family whose parents seem to hate each other more and more each day. And we have a leader that thrives on grabbing our attention by creating division. And we are a family whose children are suffering from it. P.O.G. we must be people who are together and not divided. When we stand strong in unity,and prayer there is nothing that God would not do for us. A divided house will always fall! The enemies doesn't want us to stand together,because he knows that there is power in numbers. He wants to come into your home,and destroy your family. Communication is the best way to defeat the enemy. Talk to one another about the problems you are having, then pray together about them. A family that prays together stays together. The enemy knows that if he crack the foundation of your home, which is your family, he has a good chance of destroying it. Even in war time other countries do the same they will try to attack the support systems of another country. Whenever you are able to divide something it will always break. Our leaders have taken God out of everything, school, workplace. It is time we start putting God back and believing in ourselves and showing compassion for one another again. God created us to be loving,caring and sharing with one another then no enemy can divide us.

Head Shepherd
P.O.G.
Loving Ministry

Spirit
DIVERSITY

Be the change that you wish to see in the world. The practice of quality of including or involving people from a range of different social, and ethnic backgrounds, and of different genders sexual orientation live in together in peace is all about accepting differences, and having the ability to listen to recognize respect, and appreciate others as well as living in a peaceful, and United Way. Everyone talks about peace but no one teaches peace. In this world you are educated for competition and competition is the beginning of every war. When he will educate himself for cooperation and to offer each other's solidarity. That day he will be educating himself for peace it is vital for our endurance To remember that we don't need to have all the answers. As long as we take the time to reconsider our core values, and take action towards living up to them, personal and global peace doesn't have to remain mythical unachievable point in time, instead it becomes a state of being that we can be a part of. When we as people stop seeing one another as a Color is when we will be able to come together. We are all spirits living in a human experience! Let's stop hating people who we know nothing about. overcoming the obstacles in your life will take some worrying out of your life. And let you be able to enjoy your life. Then you will see life in a different way! At this point love will be beginning to set in when you live your life with love for others. Everything around you will begin to seem much brighter.

Head Shepherd
P.O.G.
Loving Ministry

Spirit
DO IT NOW!

Genesis 9:9 I now establish my covenant with you and with your decadents after you.

Good morning People Of God family. Stop wasting time, and do what you want with your life now. Time is not on anyone's side so use it wisely. You have been putting off things trying to wait for the right moment. I believe there will never be a time when everything is perfect. Stop procrastinating just do it now. With faith, and belief you can accomplish all things with Christ. Its never to late to start over again. Don't quit the first time you don't get it right. Keep trying until you reach your goal. No one ever said it was going to be easy. It takes discipline, and consistency to achieve what you want. Stay focus, and move ahead do not let life deter you. It's in the hard times when champions are made. God has so much in store for you. Just keep believing, and it will come true. Don't let no one tell you that you cannot do this. Impossible is what faith is made of. There is no stopping you now there is power in your words. Speak victory over your life. There will be no better moment than now. God has given you dominion over the land so seize it.

Head Shepherd
P.O.G.
Loving Ministry

Spirit

DON'T GIVE UP ON ME

Jeremiah 32:27 Behold I am the Lord, the God of all flesh is there anything too hard for me?

Good morning people of God. We as people try to live a good life, but there is so much temptation in the world. We stray off the path of righteousness sometime. Letting the devil have the hold on us doing the things that are not right. Cheating, stealing, and hating people for no reason. Yet we know our heavenly father did not raise us like that. Trying to hide it from him by not telling the truth. Your father knows whats in your heart, and mind. He will never give up on you. His love is unconditional he will never turn his back on you. You must have will power to change your ways. I know the devil has a hold on you so break yourself away from him. Just ask your heavenly father to give you strength to break this hold. His laws says ask and you shall receive. Time is passing so quickly you need to be a warrior for God. So many people have giving up on their father, and living in a life of shame. The world is being ran by the devil. There are so many people who are just about themselves. Don't give up on your father. He wants you to have a life of loving, and sharing, and caring about one another. So just pray and ask him don't give up on me, and he will make you see how life can really be.

Head Shepherd
P.O.G.
Loving Ministry

Spirit
EDUCATION

Most people in life after high school they just stop wanting to learn. The mind is a terrible thing to waste. Then there are those who go to college, but when they're done they stop too. You are a creator your mind is your most powerful tool. Whatever you put into the mind it will program your life it's like a smart computer garbage in, and garbage out. So be cautious in what you put in the mind there are always new skills to learn, and strategies for you to adopt and you should never stop learning as it enables you To generate new ideas do not just stick to what you know. Learn and generate new ideas by listening, and watching out for any new resources from which you can gain new knowledge, and concepts. Learning does not end once you graduate from school as learning is a lifelong process. With that in mind you should never stop learning so you can always stay relevant, motivated, and happy. The single most important attribute to becoming more knowledgeable is self discipline. It helps you stay focused on reaching your goals gives you the function To stick with difficult task, and allows you to overcome obstacles, and discomfort as you push yourself to a new heights. When you start to develop your powers of empathy, and imagination the whole world will open up for you.. Heaven on Earth is a choice you must make, not a place you must find.

Head Shepherd
P.O.G.
Loving Ministry

Spirit
ELDERLY

Leviticus 19:32 Stand up in the presence of the aged, show respect for the elderly and revere your God. I am the Lord.

Good morning people of God. I remember when I was so happy when it was my birthday. Parties, and gifts people telling me happy birthday it was so much fun. Not a care in the world youth was on my side. I was not worried about anything just how great I felt. Then one day life set in. Marriage, family, and a new home then the years begin to past, because all you were doing is trying to take care all of these bills. You work come home sleep, and back to work again. Life start passing so quickly then one day before you know it you're old. You walk in a room, and you forget why you walked in there. Or your energy level is not what it used to be. Growing old is a pain. What happen with all these dreams you once had. Why didn't I make any of them come true for me. It's sad we cannot go back, and try again. It's time to refocus your thoughts and try again. It's never to late to grow, and be great. Your heavenly father does not want you to just live life. He wants you to enjoy life believing in yourself again. Your mind is a powerful thing have visions of being young. See yourself young again have energy eat right. You have to take care of your body. Exercise or take a walk. Your life is not done yet. God has so much more in store for you. Just believe in him, and the son. Ask him for forgiveness, and he will let you be born again. Then go out in the world, and start living again be happy, and share the good news with others. That your father loved them still. Then you will have the secret of life.

Head Shepherd
P.O.G.
Loving Ministry

Spirit
ELEVATE

Don't waste time on things you can't control. But focus on making the most of the time you do have. Today is all we have so let's live, breathe, and conduct our business with purpose for tomorrow doesn't owe us anything. Do you ever find yourself thinking negative thoughts? If so you're not alone. A lot of us tend to think negatively especially when we're stressed or depressed. Negativity and this negative mindset thinking can lead to anxiety, panic attacks, and simply is not good for your overall health, and well being. It's important to initially shift our thinking when it gets out of line. So we can live more productive and happy life. You're always in control of your own mindset and emotion and you've got the power to change them and how you feel. Elevating our lives growing as people are lifelong journeys. I believe that small intentional change can lead to big results in your life. Getting to a place where you feel secure stress free, happy and grateful can be a very rocky and difficult journey. It's a learning process you learn from. This kind of journey is by no means impossible as there are only 2 main things that you'll need to start this life course, the right mindset do not settle for an average or easy life. Never rest on your laurels or except pretty good. Safe does not equal meaningful.

Head Shepherd
P.O.G
Loving Ministry

Spirit

EMPATHY

Psalm 116.5 The Lord is gracious and righteous, our God is full of compassion.

The ability to understand and share the feelings of another. The capacity to place oneself in another position that is the only way you will understand what that person is going through. Stop being so judgmental condemning people before you have all the facts. When we are able to love someone regardless what they have done, and forgive them then we are living in our God-consciousness. Always go to sleep and wake up positive think about how to make others happy whatever you do in life stay committed, and believe in yourself. Stay committed don't miss the chance to help others you have the power to declare, and manifest anything into existence so stand in your power and do for others. Sometimes we have to stop being scared, and just be around one another. Whenever you are able to put someone else before yourself you are doing what Jesus did when he was here on this Earth. Let your heart be filled with love for all humanity. We are able to create whatever world we choose to live in. When we are able to share kindness, and love to one another then we are doing what Jesus told us. Gratitude and appreciation for others will bring happiness in your life. You can't change who you are, but you can change how you treat people. Keep your mind open and you will find the meaning of love with faith, and determination we will be able to change the world.

Head Shepherd
P.O.G.
Loving Ministry

Spirit
EFFORT

....

2 Peter 1:5 for this reason makes every effort to add to your faith excellence, to excellence, knowledge;

Good morning people of God. We are always asking God for something in life. A new job, a mate, good health and piece of mind. We then take no action so God can make it happen for us. Faith without action is dead. When you ask God for something you must believe in it. Like it has already happened, and go out in that direction. There are so many people who just sit around and wait never making any effort to do what they asked God for. If you want a better job you must start looking or training for this new position you want. There must always be some kind of effort made for what you want in life. God wants you to show him that you believe in him. By making some kind of effort to achieve what you just asked him for. Faith is believing in the unknown, and knowing that God will bring it to pass. God is a energy of positivity. You must think about the good things in life that you need. It is talking about what you want to obtain and preparing a way for it to happen for you. When you have a positive mind it is your wave link to God directly. When we are out there preparing, showing up, trying new things, contributing to our community we are more app. to stumble into something that interest us in a big way. We are more likely to learn something new, be inspired and intrigue. We are more likely to discover what drives us when we are showing up in the world. When we work at it our passion emerges. Most of us have a complicated relationship with the effort required to get things done. On the one hand, we generally prepare to do things and the easiest possible way. On the other hand, there are times when the effort we put out into accomplish a goal becomes part of the reward itself. From a biological stand point though for the most situations we are best off finding the least effortful way to achieve a goal. That is, an animal that routinely puts in a lot of effort to get some reward (say food), will be at a disadvantage relative to some other animals that puts in the least effort to get the same reward. So, we might expect that humans would have mechanisms that allows with allow amount of effort we expend to achieve a reward to affect the value we give to that reward. Whatever you want in life make some effort to make it happen for you so God can put his finger on it so you can have it.

Head Shepherd
P.O.G.
Loving Ministry

Spirit
EASY

....

Amos 6:3 you refuse to believe a day of disaster will come, but you establish a reign of violence.

Good morning people of God. We as people of God is always looking for the easy way out in life. We don't want anything to be too difficult on us. We seek jobs with the most pay, and easy labor. Our relationship must come with no problems with our mate. We even expect there to be no worries with the kids. God did not promise us an easy life. He know the devil is always busy causing chaos. Let's stop wanting everything to be easy on us. Pray and ask God to give you strength, and and ask God to give you strength to deal whatever comes your way. The times that we are in now are filled with unknowns at any moment things can go wrong. Stand strong, and let god help you fight a good fight of faith. The world is not easy anymore. We are in the end times", meaning the devil is trying to take control. Be strong, and willing to go the extra mile. It will take all you have to beat this devil. Believe in your mind that all things will work out through Christ. What really make things easy or difficult, of course it's us. Our own inner life state. When we're tired, depressed, but distracted even easy feels difficult. An when we're buoyant, unenergetic, confidence, and eager difficult feels easy. Many of us spend an inordinate amount of effort trying to avoid difficult. But what we really should be doing is seeking to strengthen ourselves so that difficult is doable. We shouldn't run from difficult. We should embrace it. As John Kennedy famously said", we didn't go to the moon because it was easy". Not to imply easy as bad or that we shouldn't enjoy it – Just that an easy life isn't only impossible, it's undesirable. Neither the human body nor the human mind were meant to be in a corner and left unused, and using both requires effort. An effort feels difficult. But effort rewards. Have a back bone, and stand up when you see things that are wrong in life. We as P.O.G must be on the front line, and be ready to fight the good fight of faith. Easy is something for the weak, and afraid people in life. We must be courageous and strong, so we can help them see the wickedness of man.

Head Shepherd
P.O.G.
Loving Ministry

Spirit
EMPOWER

Luke 9:1-6 Jesus sends out the twelve when Jesus had called the twelve together, he gave them the power and authority to drive out all demons and to cure diseases, and he sent them out to proclaim the kingdom of God to heal the sick.

There is power in the name of Jesus. Just call his name and all the enemies will flee. No darkness in hail will ever prevail over your life. Be bold and courageous to speak out about what is right. There is power in you there nothing you can not do when Jesus is with you. Stand tall don't let nothing sway you. You are the ruler of your world. Empower yourself to create your vision in life. You are the head, and not the tail you can build anything. No matter what happens in life. You will always be able to navigate your way through. You are the captain of your ship. No storm will be able to disturb you. You're on a set course to the destination you choose for your life. There is no turning back, because you're determined to finish this race. No matter how hard the winds blow your ship will sail free. The enemy will try to put doubt in your mind. But God has told him that you will make it through. There comes a time when you must believe. Even though you may not know how to make it so. Be strong in your convictions, and let God guide you. Let go and let the universal God lead you into the power within you. With your power we can defeat all the weapons of the enemy. When we get our mind to be able to think all things become possible. You are more powerful than we know. Believe this and the world become your reality.

Head Shepherd
P.O.G.
Loving Ministry

Spirit
EMPOWERMENT

Luke 9:1-6 Jesus sends out the twelve
When Jesus called the twelve together he gave them power, and authority, to drive out all demons and to cure diseases, and he sent them out to proclaim the kingdom of God and heal the sick.

We the people have been given the power to help ourselves. Yet we keep letting man tell us how to live our lives. God gave you free will to do what you wanted with your life. The process of becoming stronger and more confident, especially in controlling ones life and claiming ones rights. We are connected so, we must come together to make a difference in the world it's time to stop being afraid, and take a stand in life. Right or wrong we needed to be as one. The time has come for us to empower ourselves with God's words. Wake up every morning knowing you have the power to live your dreams. When you focus on possibilities you will have more opportunities everybody needs just a little love, lots of hope and unshakable faith. We need to get our priorities straight, and start believing in Christ. The universe has so much wonder for you to discover. You must believe in your capability to take charge over your life. The truth is that until you realize who you are your life will never change. You were made in the image of the almighty God there is power in you. You can create whatever reality you deserve. You just have to believe. When people are able to appreciate one another. Then we will be able to create a world of possibilities. Just be loving, caring and sharing with one another and let God do the rest.

Head Shepherd
P.O.G.
Loving Ministry

Spirit
ENDURE

....

Mankind is often troubled by the future. Our imagination can run wild and devise horrible doomsday scenarios and dystopia futures. Scientists theorize about multiple events that could end the world As we know it. He who endures to the end shall be safe. This promise should be encouraging to God's people, and fill us with hope. God's people who faithfully endure everything will be given the gift of salvation eternal life in the family of god! With the religion deception, warfare, famine, pestilence, and a natural disaster striking all over the world, people will turn against the people of God. In their anger and confusion mankind will lash out against anyone. Trying to live by God's ways. Neighbors and family will betray one another. In this era of lawlessness people will lose love for one another. All illusions of civility will disappear in the world. That appears to be falling apart. Knowing that his time is almost up, Satan will attack God's people with everything he has. Know your power, the more power you have create in the universe in your existence. Be accountable know yourself live just to live with a higher awareness of who you are. More importantly, who you are, not. P.O.G. we need to come together and fight back to keep control of this world. God has promised no weapons shall ever be formed against us, find your way. Find your energy and work these things out with others. So we can all brighten up this world together".

Head Shepherd
P.O.G.
Loving Ministry

Spirit
ENJOYMENT

Psalms37:3 Trust in the Lord and do good, dwell in the land and enjoy safe pasture.

Good morning People of God. I say why do people go through life always upset about something? We live our lives always working, worrying, and complaining about things. Just running this rat race trying to get ahead. All that stress with make you sick! Learn to relax and just chill out. You live half of your life working isn't it time to start enjoying yourself? Take time, and smell the roses in life. Stress, and worry no more leave God in charge of your life. Take time to enjoy the creations God has already given you. The lakes, parks, and the mountains there is so much beauty in his work. It doesn't take much to enjoy life. Its all in your mind how you precieve it have a vision of splendor. There is so much to do all around you, and it cost you nothing. Look at life through the eyes of a child. Be young again let your imagination run wild. Life is what you make it so make it something great. There is no time like the present to start living a wonderful life. When you live for God that is a good start.

Head Shepherd
P.O.G.
Loving Ministry

Spirit
ENOUGH

Smart people learn from everything and everyone, average people from their experiences, and stupid people already have all the answers. At which point in your life will you say enough? We are going through storms in life. You have to stop accepting the status quo.. You are more than average you have the ability to do whatever you want in life. Don't let anyone tell you that you can't. Enough already stand up and be someone. You have the power in you to determine your life. We all have our breaking point. There is a point when enough truly is enough. It's different for each one of us, and obviously depends on the circumstances. If you feel like you're been Over extending yourself or reaching a climatic breaking point with someone then you will know when it is time to say no more. We as human beings tend to idolize things we want. You have to make a choice how you want to live your life. Be around people that you can learn from people who want more out of life. People who are stretching, and searching, and seeking some higher ground in life. At the end of the day life is a fight for territory. And once you stop fighting for what you want what you don't want will automatically take over. At some point we need to say enough is enough and I deserve better. You can start to imagine what you want in life. Start with a re evaluation of core values focus on them, and use them to guide your next move. Every choice consider can be checked against the core values to be sure the decision are in alignment with what you value most in life.

Head Shepherd
P.O.G.
Loving Ministry

Spirit
EXPECTATIONS

Psalms 84:11 For the Lord God is a sun and shield: the Lord will give grace and glory: no good thing will withhold from them that walk uprightly.

Good morning people of God. Why do people in the world today live their lives never expecting nothing good will happened to them. They live their lives day to day not once believing that there is greatness with in them. If you want greatness you must think that you are the greatest. Stop letting the enemy fool you into believing that you are average. There is power with in you. With faith you can tap into it. God has made you to do all things when you believe it is time to change your thoughts, and start believing in your self again. Whatever you want in life speak it into existence. There is so much you can have in life with God on your side. Your father wants you to live a life of abundance. Pray each and every day ask him to show you the way. We often we began our adult years with high hopes, and visionary dreams for our future. Along the way most of us experience a lost of spirit as we endure broken relationships, and shattered dreams. When we look for strength and hope in our selfishness, and sin filled world, and or with in our own fragile selves, we invariably end up disappointed or disillusioned we lose hope and lose heart. Expect good things to happened to you each and everyday. Wellness, greatness and happiness isn't far away. Expect these things for your life. God is so awesome he will feed the hunger make the blind see. You must believe he can do this for thee. There is nothing impossible for God. So expect it for you.

Head Shepherd
P.O.G.
Loving Ministry

Spirit
EYES WIDE OPEN

Psalm119:18 Open my eyes that I may see wonderful things in your law.

Good morning people of God. Have you ever seen a car accident happen right in front of you? You see the hold thing unfold right before your eyes. Wondering why the drivers are unaware of what is about to happen. You want to warn them by blowing your horn, or yelling out. We see things in life all the time that are bad, but yet we do nothing to help that person out. We feel like we don't want to get involved with it. Try to look away at what is happening right in front of us. The Devil has us so afraid, and scared to help someone who is hurting. God is a father with compassion in his heart. He will not let any harm come to you when you are doing his will. Stop letting the devil win all the time take some action, and help others in need. When there isn't any fear in your heart all things can become possible again. There isn't nothing you wouldn't try or do. Be bold, and courageous and step out on faith, and be the person God created you to be. Lets be people who's eyes are wide open with a heart of compassion for others. Loving, caring, and sharing with one another. We are all blessed by God. But there may come a time when you will need someone there for you. What a person sow is what they will reap. Meaning do good for others so that good will always happen for you.

Head Shepherd
P.O.G.
Loving Ministry

Spirit
FANTASTIC

Proverbs 15:30 Light in a messenger's eyes brings joy to the heart, and good news gives health to the bones.

When you are able to have a spirit of good vibrations your life will be filled with awesomeness. A positive outlook on life will attract good things. Stay filled with the Holy Spirit go through life with an attitude of thankfulness. Be loving toward those you meet in life you can change the mood of the day by touching someone's heart with your smile. Sometimes you don't even realize you're blocking your own blessings by holding on to the pass or thinking negativity. Have A unbelievable life by being positive all the time when you live a fantastic life things will be all right. If you are surrounded by those who love your ambition you'll be more ambitious and achieve more. People are attracted to happy people it is better to be lonely than allowed people who are not going anywhere keep you from your destiny. Don't let fear keep you from living your best life now. No labels, no fear, no darkness. I am love you are love all humanity need unity of Peace & Love, and we will change the world. What you think about becomes your reality be grateful send out vibrations of love be happy! Allow your heart the space it needs to manifest your highest desires in to existence. When you really just let things be and detach from all outcomes you give life the opportunity and space to work in your favor.

Head Shepherd
P.O.G.
Loving Ministry

Spirit
FELLOWSHIP

We as spiritual believers need to come together. To be able to transform this world into the reality we choose. We are all spiritually connected to the universal God. We all have ideas that we can share. In order to be able to help, and care for one another when you stop thinking just about yourself that is when you are connecting to your true powers. Have an attitude, of forgiveness, gratitude, and joyful to help humanity. Never show a sign of weakness to the enemy. Even though you may be going through the storm. Your point of power is in the now moment. When we are able to stop looking at the past, and the future and live in a now moment. That is when we are able to create a better world. There is only one way to happiness, and that is to cease worrying about things which are beyond the power of our will. We all need one another in order to change the ways of the world. Fellowship is something that keeps us all moving forward the measure of intelligence is the ability to change. Change how you look at people, and start seeing them as someone of importance. You can't change the past, but you can change the future, and that starts in the present moment. Our thoughts are frequencies that connect us to the universal God. We should all have thoughts of greatness, abundance, at all times. When we are all together with the same thoughts on the same frequency that is when we can manifest the world we see.

Head Shepherd
P.O.G.
Loving Ministry

Spirit
FERTILIZE

You need to fertilize your spirit with positive thoughts. Have good things to say about the people around you. Show respect to everyone you meet and know. Be a Beacon of light, and let others see the good in you. Every living thing needs love to be spoken to in order to grow. You will always attract more bees with honey not vinegar. Spiritual growth is a process of shedding our wrong and unreal concepts, thoughts, beliefs in ideas and becoming more conscious and aware of our inner being. Spiritual growth is the process of inner awakening rising of the consciousness beyond the ordinary everyday existence, and awakening to some universal truth. It means going beyond the mind and the ego, and realizing who you really are. You were made in the image of the Almighty God. With your belief all things become possible you can create whatever It means going beyond the mind and the ego and realizing who you really are. You were made in the image of the Almighty God. With your belief all things become possible you can create whatever reality you choose to live in. Your thoughts are your creative power. Think of greatness to achieve the impossible. Every new beginning starts from a fertilizing moment. Keep the weeds out by not having negative thoughts.. Most great accomplishments were achieved by the people who at 1st had no idea what they were doing. Personal growth is not a matter of learning new information but unlearning old limits.

Head Shepherd
P.O.G.
Loving Ministry

Spirit
FIGHT

Exodus 14:14 The Lord will fight for you: you need only to be still.

Good morning people of God, Why don't people be willing to fight for what they believe in any more. They are so afraid to speak out about what is wrong in society today. You will never have anything worth having if you don't stop being scared. Some things in life you must fight for. Like your kids, your family, and better health. The devil don't want you to have these things. You must make a stand and be willing to battle for this. The enemy don't fight fair. He will do anything to defeat you. You must fight like your life depend on it. You have to know that god is there with you right by your side. Blow for blow he will help you win the good fight of faith. Believe in your strength and capability of winning. The time has come for us all to battle this enemy before he takes over the world again. Plead to God "fight against those who fight against me." we need all P.O.G. nation to be ready when duty calls for us to fight. We are conquerors with Christ.

Head Shepherd
P.O.G.
Loving Ministry

Spirit FRIENDS

Proverbs 17:17 A friend loves at all times, and a relative is born to help in adversity.

Good morning people of God. Each friend represent a world in as, a world possibly not born until they arrive, and it is only by the meeting that a new world is born. All people of God have friends in their life some good and some bad. A true friend is someone who will be there by your side through all the storms of life. Unconditional love is what a true friend should have for you, it should be like a marriage between both of you share, comfort, and listen to each other. It should always be that both of you will be there for each other no matter what. God knows who is right for you in your life. If you would just ask him. Some of us have hundreds of friends but just evaluate them and see if they will be there if you are sick or in jail and come to visit you. We put too much faith in some of our friends when we shouldn't, because in the end we winde up being disappointed and hurt by them. A friend is someone who believes in what you do and that should be Godly. With God in your relationship you can never go wrong. Friendship is about being equal in the way you help each other. It should never be one is always giving and never receiving. A friend is someone who will be mad at you but you make up real soon. Forgiveness is a trait of a true friend. A friend may not always agree with you but they will respect your opinion. They will never talk about you behind your back, but uplift you to others when they can. A true friend is someone you can depend on no matter what is going on in your life. You may have many friends but there are few you can call a true friend. So make sure when you are calling others your friend make sure they are those who have your back at all times. God has placed people in your life to keep you on a path of righteousness. He has also given you free will to choose the right ones as your friends. If you want a real friend ask Jesus to be your friend. No one has greater love, no one has shown stronger affection then to lye down (give up his own life for his friends) CHOOSE WISELY MY FRIEND!

Head Shepherd
P.O.G.

Spirit
FAMILY VALUES

Romans 16:19 For while your loyalty and obedience I known to all, so that I rejoice over you, I would have you well versed and wise as to what is good and innocent and guileless as to what is evil.

Good morning People of God. My friend for life is a person named Sharlene Brooks. Her grandmother just recently passed. I sent all my sorrows to her and her family members. They took care of her grandmother. They took her grandmother in when she was bedridden and not able to help herself anymore. Loyal to her till the end of life that was 11 years making sure all her needs were met by feeding, bathing, and dressing her, taking her to all her doctor's appointments.

There was someone always there day or night to watch over her. Her grandmother was like a newborn baby again. Would you do this for your family member if asked of you?

There are many who would just walk away from the situation and leave it for someone else to do like a nursing home or another family member.

In China it is customary for kids to take care of their elderly parents. We should do this the same way here in America. I applaud them, No, I salute them. They are all what we need to be, caring, compassionate, God fearing God loving people. This family's heart and conscience are in the right place.

Jesus said to love your enemy and hate none.

Your family values and definitions consist of ideas passed down from generation to generation. It boils down to philosophy of how you want to live your family life. Our social values are often times reinforced by our spiritual or religious beliefs and traditions. Traditionally, people define their values as stating that the family comes first, yet they find themselves with very little time or energy left over for spending time with their family.

Hopefully, you have instilled some family values into your family so that when you are elderly your family will be there for you doing what this family did for theirs. May God, mercy and grace be over all of you.

Head Shepherd
POG

Spirit FOCUS

Psalm 34:10 The young lions do lack, and suffer hunger, but they that seek the Lord shall not want any good things.

Good morning P.O.G. family. We as people of God always loose focus on what we want to do in life. Whenever we are trying to do what is right in Life the enemy always try to make us loose focus. Why is that? I believe he knows what our weakness are in life. We are always trying to take a short path instead of trying to stay on a path of righteousness trying to achieve quick wealth. My mom once told me easy come easy goes. To have anything good in life you must stay focus on it until you have it. Your thought process is a wave link to God he hears you. So have thoughts of greatness. Whenever you focus on something good your father will make it happen for you. We as people sometime want it right away, and stop focusing on it. God said everything has its season to come to you. Remember the people of Egypt wondered forty years in the wilderness to get to the promise land. Gods time frame, and our time frame is much different. When we dwell on past events too much, then we are unable to hear god calling us into the future. When we ignore past events to focus on the future the worst parts of history often repeats themselves. Be focus on the good qualities of life like caring and sharing, and loving with someone. Then all your dreams will come to past.

Head Shepherd
P.O.G.
Loving Ministry

Spirit
FOLLOW YOUR HEART

Job 9:4 He is wise in heart, and mighty in strength who hath hardened himself against him, and hath prospered.

Good morning people of God. Why are people in the world today so afraid to follow their hearts anymore? I believe its, because someone in the pass has used, and abused them. It has become difficult for them to trust anymore. Your heart knows what is right or wrong to do in life. You were deceived by the enemy in your mind that is why you went down the wrong path. The heart is good, but the mind can be corrupted or deceived. Your heart is filled with so many emotions love, hate, envy, but you must decide on which one to follow. God has placed love in your heart just listen to him. We all should have compassion for people in life. You see the sick, the hungry, and sad people. Does your heart ache. This is God talking to you to do something about it. Have you ever did something good for someone, and it made your heart feel better? The best prescription for your heart ache is loving,and sharing, and caring for someone. This organ is life so why not enjoy your life. By spending time with others. Coming together to worship our heavenly father, and pray for one another.

Head Shepherd
P.O.G.
Loving Ministry

Spirit

FREE WILL

....

John 8:32 Then you will know the truth, and the truth will set you free.

Good morning people of God. God has placed free will in all of us, meaning that you can do what is right in life. He has left it all up to you to do what is right. There are so many people who cannot rationalize what is right or wrong. We are people who see so much on TV, social media, or hear what is going on in life. We think we are doing the right thing because, we see others doing it. The children of the world today are raised in a one parent home. There is never anyone there to raised them right. We live in a monkey see, monkey do society. Thinking others know what is the right thing to do in life. The free will debate has long been the domain of philosophers, but in recent years, neuro scientist, and psychologist have entered the fray to try to understand the brain's role in free will. Several seminal neurological studies, for instance, have concluded that the brain lights up with activity several seconds before a person becomes consciously aware of a decision, which some argue is an indication that people don't have free will, and that human actions are just the product of internal electrical activity. Others argue, however, that a freely-made choice simply triggers the brain's activity before an individual is consciously aware of it. Keep your mind waves set on the goodness of God and compassion for others. Then whatever you decide to do in life it will always turn out right.

Head Shepherd
P.O.G.
Loving Ministry

Spirit
FRESH START

1 John 2:7 Dear friends, I am not writing you a new command but an old one, which you have had since the beginning. This old command is the message you have heard.

Good morning my P.O.G. family. Its that time of year to begin a new again. We all want to make a fresh start at the beginning of a new year. Trying to do what is right in life, loose weight, eat right, or go back to school. We are going to make it happen this time. Our hopes are high we dream big. We are filled with an inspiration we are driven. We need to be more focus this time. You must have clarity on what you want to accomplish. Then with discipline, and consistency you can make this happen. God wants you to achieve your dreams on being a better person. Difficult times will come but stay prayed up, and ask your father for guidance. What ever you think about you can do those things. Believe in yourself. Stay committed until you reached your goal. There will be some people who don't want you to be better than them. They will not be in your corner. It will be some of your closest friends. Don't let them stop you from being all you can be. Sometimes you must weed your garden by cutting them off. Its hard enough already you don't need anyone telling you you cannot do this. Whenever you are close to reaching your goal that is when the enemy is working hard to stop you. Know that God is on your side he wants you to have the good things in life. STAY FOCUS and ACHIEVE.

Head Shepherd
P.O.G.
Loving Ministry

Spirit FRUSTRATION

Ephesians 4:26 In your anger do not sin, do not let the sun go down while you are still angry.

Good morning people of God. Why do we sometime go through life keeping things bottled up inside us? Just holding on to it until we are ready to explode. Striking out at everyone around us not realizing that every action has a reaction. Now you have caused,or hurt to someone you did not intend to hurt. There are no do overs in life. We need to learn to let go, and let god in our life. Whenever you have a misunderstanding with someone you need to talk it over with them. There is no problem you cannot solve with God in it. Just have faith God can rectify all things when you have God in it. The world is filled with so much ciaos why would you want more in your life. There is no situation that two people cannot redeem when they compromise. No two can be right so why fight. Let God in your life to be your judge, and your jury. Men have been at war for centuries, and yet they still don't understand Gods power. There is no pain or sorrow that God cannot take care of. Stop being upset about everything in life. There is hope when you have faith believe in the impossible.

Head Shepherd
P.O.G.
Loving Ministry

Spirit
GIFT TO GAB

I Samuel 2:3 Do not keep talking so proudly or let your mouth speak such arrogance, for the lord is a God who knows, and by him deeds are weighed.

Good morning people of God. There are so many people who can go on, and on talking about anything in life. They can be so articulate about the subject they are talking about. On and on they go talking only to take a breath every now and then. Do you know someone like this? Its not the talking its the message they are giving. Is it informative, or teaching, is it helping others? I believe you should use this gift to teach others. Most people are scared to speak to a group of people with elegance. When you are trying to uplift, and encourage people in life your father is there with you. Make sure you are building up people, and not tearing them down. Speak words of encouragement make them believe in themselves again. We all have something that has made our life better stop being a hoarder of the information, and share it with others so that it may help them also. Whenever you are trying to convey something to others, and you do not have the confidence just ask your heavenly father to give you the words to speak. There are so many that talks like politicians, lawyers and sales people telling us things that will benefit them only. Its time to stop giving lip service and start talking about the goodness of God.

Head Shepherd
P.O.G.
Loving Ministry

Spirit

GREATFULNESS

Timothy 1:12 I am grateful to the one who has strengthened me, Christ Jesus our lord because he considered me faithful in putting me into ministry.

Season greetings "!! We as people of god don't appreciate the little things in life that god do for us. Each morning we wake up and not once we are grateful for god letting us see another day.

We have shelter to keep us warm and lay our heads. There is something in the refrigerator to eat and you have clothes to put on your body. Be grateful for the little things god do for you praise him and give thanks to your heavenly father. Our body function works well we can see beauty in the world,and yet we are not grateful still. God has given you Family and love ones to be around but we still complain how bad things are. Be grateful for what he has given you. BECAUSE OTHERS MAY NOT HAVE WHAT YOU DO, and someone else will love to be in your shoes. Be grateful with the little things then maybe god can trust you with more blessings if you just appreciate what you have already. Remember grateful people of god act less aggressively because thinking and acting in grateful ways requires empathy for others.

Head Shepherd
P.O.G

Spirit
GO FOR IT

2 Kings 8:2 The woman proceeded to do as the man of God said, she and her family went away and stayed in the land of the philistines seven years.

Good morning people of God. We as P.O.G. must not be scared to go for what you want in life. God has promised us greater things in life, if we believe in the son. Stop being afraid, and start thinking there is greatness in you. Believe in yourself step out in faith, and go after for what you want in life. Be that risk taker, and just go for it. You will never know if you never go for it you could have received it. We as people just sit around, and wait hoping things will go our way. You must be strong, and take some action, to make your life the way you desire it to be. Don't let anyone tell you your not able to go for it. Have a mindset that you can go for whatever you want in life. Just go for it no matter what stands in your way. Have the ability to move around any obstacles in life. Pray and ask your father he will show you the way. The enemy do not want you to have what God has promised you already. It is never to late in life to go for what you believe in. There is no sin, no badness, no shame that the father will not forgive you of. Just go for it and ask him to cleanse your heart, and make you whole again so life will be a new beginning again. Just go for it then you will see how beautiful things can be.

Head Shepherd
P.O.G.
Loving Ministry

Spirit

GOING THROUGH

We are all put here on this planet to go through different experiences in life. Good or bad it's not how you go through them, but how you come out of them. You are being tested to be able to control your emotions. The enemy knows if he can keep you in a negative energy that you will fail. It's very important to keep your emotions balanced good or bad. That is why the universal God says you must be able to forgive. Proverbs chapter 17 verse 9 love prospers when a fault is forgiven, but dwelling on it separates close friends. If we confess our sins, he is faithful and just to forgive us, and to cleanse us from all unrighteousness, stop looking for validation, and other opinions of you. Know thyself and love who you are. Everyone who tries to do big things will go through the struggle appreciate the struggle that's where the growth comes. Whether you're facing a global or personal crisis or a mix of both building resilience can help you cope with stress, overcome adversity, and enjoy better days to come. Difficult times can take a heavy toll on your mood, health, and outlook. It can leave you filling helpless, and overwhelmed by stress and anxiety. Connecting with friends and family when you're going through tough times can help ease stress, boost your mood, and make sense of all the change, and disruption. The people you reach out to don't need to have answers to the problem you're facing they just need to be willing to listen to you without judging. Is the human connection eye contact, a smile, or a hug that can make all the difference to how you're feeling.

Head Shepherd
P.O.G
Loving Ministry

Spirit
GOOD PEOPLE!

Psalm 133:1 How good and pleasant it is when Gods people live together in unity.

In order to have a happy life you must surround ourselves with good people. People who are able to uplift, and encourage us in life. Someone with positive attitude. Have you ever notice someone with a smile on their face most of the time? These are the types of people you should be around. When someone is upbeat it can be contagious. Just imagine having the ability of being joyful all the time. No worries or regrets in life. Your heart will be ad ease, and your mind will be at peace. When your able to have this type of calm in your life the world will look much different. All the problems in life will just flow away. You will be able to make rational decisions about your life. People around you will begin to wonder how is it you are so calm. They will see something amazing about you and they will want to be in your shoes. When we are able to live our lives with love in our hearts the world we be more of a beautiful place. Good people are those who can manifest their reality. The secret to the universe is love. When we are able to do this you can have your heart desires. Start seeing goodness in people stop focusing on the things we cannot control, but focus on the good in people. It matters how you treat people, because how you treat them they will do you the same for you. Show compassion for everyone in your life. You have to become that good person inside of you to make a difference in someones life let this become habit forming". Good peoples are who God created us to be show love, caring, and sharing, with each other then we will be able to change the world.

Head Shepherd
P.O.G.
Loving Ministry

Spirit
GIVE THANKS

Psalms 100:4 Enter his gates with thanksgiving and his courts with praise; give thanks to him and praise his name.

I know it seems the world has been turned upside down. That everything bad is good is just the enemy is trying to make it that way. Be thankful for all the good in your life. Your able to walk, talk, and see the beauty in the world. Be grateful for what God has done. Keep your joy it could have been much worse off. Listen to your inner peace remain calm in any situation. This world is filled with such sadness. Don't let it take your happiness. Wake up each day living in the moment. Knowing your going to take control of your day. Give thanks for what God has done for all the little things in your life. Live life, loving everyone, and put a smile on your face no matter what the enemy has done. He has no authority over your life. When you are grateful for the little things your father will always give you more in life. Don't be materialistic but be compassionate about life. Always listen to your heart it will guide you into paradise. Whenever you are content you are beginning to know the secret of life.

Head Shepherd
P.O.G.
Loving Ministry

Spirit

GROWING

....

Peter2:2 and yearn like newborn infants for pure, spiritual milk so that by it you may grow up salvation.

Good morning people of God. We as people of God have stop growing in Gods words and his laws. We have let society dictate to us they way we should live our lives even the government is being ran by the devil telling us how we should live. There isn't any godliness in the way you live then you are not doing what he asked for you to do. We have taken his words and his laws out of everything in life. We have stopped growing from being people of excellence, and always willing to help others. America was built on the words and the laws of the bible even slaves believed in God and followed his laws. When there is no God in what you do in life then it will never work to your advantage. God must be present to achieve what you want in life. We must start growing again by doing God's will. We must believe in the sun and turn back the hands of time back to when the nation is under Gods laws. We as a nation have stop growing being prosperous and being great because we let men tell us how to live. We must continue to grow in Gods words, like our garden does if you want things to be better in your community like your garden you must weed it like your community stop the violence. You must mulch it like your garden stop the murdering in your communities and you must give it living water. Like your community you must uplift and love one another. We have stop growing because we don't pray over our family like our mother did. If we want to do better in life we must read the bible more and pray more and do his commandments then we will grow and be stronger and be able to take back our community. Then the enemy will know you will stand for no more. Violence, murdering, hating, then society will start to progress in the right way. Without God in your life there will never be any peace no joy and definitely no peace of mind we need to start growing again BY LOVING EACH OTHER AND HAVING PASSION FOR HUMANITY. Just read your bible and be around other people of God and follow his laws. It isn't hard to do try it and see. Then you will be healthy and whole again standing tall above all others. God word is something you can believe in he will never let you stop growing. Now have faith trust in God and following Gods direction in order to help others.

Head Shepherd
P.O.G.

Spirit
GRACE

....

Ephesians 2:8-9 For it is by grace you have been saved, through faith- and this is not from yourselves, it is the gift of God- not by works, so that no one can boast.

When we are able to be grateful in life that is when we appreciate the things in life. There is so much positive energy in knowing your purpose in life. God is shown grace on us to create a peaceful world. No one can take this away from us. When we believe that is when all things become possible. It's important to surround ourselves with positive people. There are no limitation with God's everything is possible. Let go of your past mistakes, and try something different it is crucial not to be Judgmental of ourselves. Having a worry free attitude is your Christ conscience. Be thankful for all that God has done he has given you all your needs in life to be yourself in a world that is consistently trying to make you something else, is the greatest accomplishment. Sometimes you gotta let go of who you were so that you can become who God-created you to be, to achieve your goals, and, ambitions. You already have what it takes to live the life you choose. Life is not what you want it, what you make it. Believe God wants you to live a wonderful life. When we all can let go of our differences in life then we will be able to connect with each other. On a higher level when we are able to let love guide us we will never go astray.

Head Shepherd
P.O.G.
Loving Ministry

Spirit
GUILTY BY ASSOCIATION

Exodus 34:7 Keeping mercy for thousands, forgiving iniquity and transgression and sin and that will by no means clear the guilty, visiting the iniquity of the fathers upon the children, and upon the children's children, unto the third and to the fourth generation.

Good Morning People of God. How can we as a people, God, stop the violence in the world if we are so afraid to speak out against it when we see it happening?

God said, let no weapon form against us prosper. That means he will protect you from being harmed. People see bad things happen to other people, but they just close their eyes and pretend they don't see it happening.

You know you are as guilty as the people who did the crime if you don't say anything to the authorities. This is what happened in Germany when Hitler started taking over other countries. He wasn't concerned about it until it came to their country being taken over. If you don't stop evil at the beginning, it will grow and spread. Bad people begin to think it's all right to hurt the good people. So we must stand together to defeat the bad in life by speaking out against it when it happens. Because in unity, there is strength.

When we pray together, we have faith in the father to bring us through our problems in life.

There are good people who have friends that are bad people. And they know about the bad things they are doing to the good people in life. But they think they are doing their bad friend a favor by not telling about the wrong that person is doing in life.

You should want to help them save their soul and stop them from hurting other people. If you are not telling them the error of their ways, it's like you are helping them to hurt the good person they are after.

All communities are filled with violence and crime. We know who are doing some of them, but yet, we look away hoping someone from the outside will help us to make our community safe.

They don't care because they don't live there. It is up to us to take some action by speaking out and saying NO MORE. THIS IS IT.

We need soldiers of God to help stop the madness in the world today. People when you stand up to evil, then God is on your side. With him you can defeat all things. Let the bad people know we will not stand for no further killing or hurting of God's people.

Then elected officials will see we care about our community and we are in numbers. Then they will listen to us and help us out.

It only takes one person to make a stand, then the others will follow their lead. People, let's be bold and courageous to speak out about the violence, to stop the hurting of God's people. Fear is just another way the devil likes you to feel so he can keep you from God's grace and mercy. Your community should be providing blessing and wholeness for everyone. BE THAT SOLDIER OF GOD.

Head Shepherd
POG

Spirit GRIT

....

Psalm 27:14 Wait for the Lord; be strong and take heart and wait for the Lord.

Courage, and resolve, strength, of character is some of the things you should believe about yourself in order to change your life. You must first change the way you think about yourself. Jesus said in order for a man to help others he must first love himself growth, and change is painful, but nothing is painful as being stuck where you don't belong. You cannot control what happened to you you can only control how you respond to them. We have to change the way we look at reality, and stop believing that we can't make a difference in this world. If we just took the time to see the good in others then we will begin to understand each other. No one is without sin so we must stop judging each other. Jesus said those without sin let them be the first to throw the stone. God has placed love in everyone's heart it's up to us to follow his words. When we are able to have courage and follow God's words. That is when we will be able to build character in ourselves. This world will always tell you that you are not good enough. But don't believe this enemy, because God chose you to be the person who help and serve others. Don't tell others of your capability, but show them instead with action. Becomes so focused that everything around you that is not moving You towards your goal becomes eventually silence. Truly spiritual people are teachers teach yourself to care about everyone You towards your goal becomes eventually silence.

Head Shepherd
P.O.G
Loving Ministry

Spirit
HEART

The 2 most important things in life. Is love God and yourself with all your heart and soul. Focus on yourself, and do what you love, and work hard into achieve your goals. Good hearted people are the ones that care about others, and do good deeds. They want to make the world a better place. They are often overlook for their good deeds, but they deserve recognition. But today we will dive into the traits of good hearted people. Good hearted people know how to emphasize with other feeling. They understand what someone is going through, and help them in any way they can. They don't judge or give up on someone, because they are having a hard time. They will be there for them until the end. They will respect the need, and wants of the people around them, and accept them for the way they are, instead of trying to change them. They will not discriminate amongst people on the basis of religion, or skin color, or nationality. A person with a good heart is the one who is open to expressing love, and emotion. They lift others up when needed and show kindness. Good hearted people accept good heart people Into their lives. Our purpose here on this Earth is to be loving, sharing and caring for one another. When you're living the life the way you are supposed to there will always be more sunny days and not rain. Either you run the day or the day runs you. To be yourself in a world that is constantly trying to make you something else is the greatest accomplishment.

Head Shepherd
P.O.G.
Loving Ministry

Spirit
HAPPINESS

Job 7:7 Remember that my life is but a breath, that my eyes will never again see happiness.

Good morning people of God. We as people of God would love to be happy 24 hours a day. It is just that life situations keep making us upset or mad all the time. The devil knows if you are sad more than happy. He can keep you under his wings. Total happiness is a God trait that is why it is so hard for many to do all the time. When you are happy it comes with peace of mind also, meaning you can think more clearly and do the right thing. True happiness is having a positive attitude. And not being negative all the time. God is in charge pray and meditate on his words daily will make this happen for you. Total happiness will also cure you of some of your health problems like depression. Being in good spirit means the Lord is with you, so nothing bad can happen to you. In all your thoughts throughout the day let them be happy. You must love yourself first then feel good about whatever you are doing in life. Happiness is a total belief in God knowing that he is always there by your side. Money is not the only thing to make you happy. Money buys freedom from worry about the basics- Housing, food, clothing. Life circumstance achievements. Marital status, social relationship, evens your neighbors all influence how happy you are or can be. Happiness is a decision you make, not an emotion you feel. This is a day the Lord has made we will rejoice and be glad in it. Having God first in your life and believing there is something better, by doing for others. Then he will give you total peace of mind with no more worrying about things in life. Then you will know true happiness.

Head Shepherd
P.O.G.

Spirit
HOME TRAINING

....

Matthew 3:9 And do not think you can say to yourselves we have Abraham as our father. I tell you that out of these stones God can raise up children for Abraham.

Good morning people of God. People in today's society don't home train their kids as well as the old timers did. These millennial are out of control! Some are lazy others don't know how to speak to people with respect. My mother once said it takes a village to raise a child. Nowadays it is only one parent house holds. These kids need a man, and a dad to raise them. Its hard for one person trying to be two persons. A lady cannot train a boy to be a man, and a man cannot train a girl to become a woman. It takes both parent to raise a child. Most of us just let social media raise our kids. At the age of one we buy them a cellphone,and give them a tablet. And from then on that's all we see them on. Social media is being controlled by the devil so you can imagine how your child will turn out to be. The kids are so quick to call the authorities when you try to discipline them. So you don't because you are afraid of the devil. Parents you cannot be a friend with your child. You must be the leader,and show them the ways of Christ. You cannot make your child happy all the time. There are times when they do wrong you must discipline them, And not with a time out. Tough love is the best love. You need to train them so they will know life is not fair. There are bad times in life, and they must learn how to deal with them. You take them to a doctor,and they just put them on pills. Then they are labeled for life with bipolar disorder,or A.D.D. Your kids are not mad or crazy it just the devil has a hold on them, because you let him raise them. " It's time to break that hold! God has promised you if you ask him he will help you. There are no bad kids but just bad teachers. If you trained them up from a baby you will see what a difference it will be. A child is going to do what they see or hear. So train them in Gods ways. I know this world is filled with so much corruption. You must believe God is there for you just ask him for some guidance.

Head Shepherd
P.O.G
Loving Ministry

Spirit
HELPFULNESS

Genesis 2:13 Get up! Help the boy up and hold him by the hand, for I will make him into a great nation.

Good morning people of God. We as people of God all need help from others at some point in life when things start going bad. We need people of God to encourage us to hold on to the faith and know things will be better. God will never leave you at your weakest moment, it is then he is holding on to you the tightest. The devil will never pull you out of Gods arms because, God loves you too much. We as people all need some kind of help with our finance, marriage, health, and education. People of God must be willing to help someone in need even if you don't know them. God says he will always reward those who help the least of thee. Helping someone is not always about giving them money; you can offer your time or just lend a hand or ear. There is something in ever people of God. You can offer to help others. God has placed a gift or talent in all of us that we can share with others. Help is something that most people do not want to ask for because of their pride. Pride will never feed you or help you with the difficulties in life. Asking someone for help is not showing weakness but know God is in others to help you through life problems. That's why it's better to think in terms of being "helpful" for somebody. None of us is perfect, we all have our quirks, and differences, and each of us is unique with our own needs and desires. It doesn't matter how your strengths and weaknesses measure out in the balances what matter is how they help other people.

Head Shepherd
P.O.G.

Spirit
HUMAN

God created all people equally. Good morning people of God. God created all humans to taste, see, smell, hear, and touch. He did not create anyone from being different from anyone else. God created all humans in his image. There is no one better than anyone else we are all equal. Our bodies have the same organs brains, heart, and intestines. We eat, think, sleep alike. Why do we have a problem with color? God created all things with different colors. The flowers, the leaves on the trees, and even the fish in the sea. They don't have a problem getting along. We as people has made it necessary to disagree thinking we are better than others. Through out times there has always been another race thinking they are superior. There has been so much blood shed over racism. God created all men equal why we just can't all get along? Is it possible for someone to hate you over the color of your skin? Or is it something deeper? I believe racism stems from hate, because they don't understand who you are. We are all a child of God. Even the bible says tho should not hate. Racism is self taught. So stop teaching hate, and start teaching to love one another.

Head Shepherd
P.O.G.
Loving Ministry

Spirit

HUMOR

The quality of being amusing or comic, especially as expressed in literature, or speech. Laughter is good for the soul it helps you to live old. You don't have to be great to start, but you have to start to be great! Smile in the face of negative, and anything or anyone that has negative in it. Keep moving forward in life and reach all that A confident, and positive warrior puts their mind to. When it comes to relieving stress more giggles, and sufferance are just what the doctor ordered. Whether you're guffawing at a sitcom and TV or quietly giggling at a newspaper article, cartoon laughing does you good. Laughter is a great form of stress relief. And that's no joke, A good sense of humor can't cure-all elements, but data is mounting about the positive things laughter can do. AA good laugh has great short-term effects when you start to laugh. It doesn't just lighten your load mentally. It actually induces physical change in your body. It's true laughter is strong medicine. It draws people together, and weighs that trigger healthy physical. Any emotional changes in the body. Laughter strengthens your immune system, boost mood, diminishes pain, and protects you from the damaging effects of stress. Nothing works faster or more dependable to bring your mind, and body back into balance then a good laugh. Humor lightens your burdens, inspires hope, connect you to others, and keeps you grounded focus and, alert It also helps you release anger, and forgive sooner. Accept responsibility for your life. Know that it is you who will get you where you want to go, no one else.

Head Shepherd
P.O.G.
Loving Ministry

Spirit
I AM

....

Everyone has their bad time at some point in life. We feel defeated and down by all the obstacles that interfere with our comfortable life. Some things don't go well the way we want sometime we see betrayal. In any case it shouldn't stop. We have to stay strong and never give up. You must believe that everything in life is possible and not impossible. Tell yourself I am a warrior and I will not stop until I have what I desire. Sell yourself everyday on your belief that what you will achieve for that day. You need to make things happen no matter what the obstacles may be. I am somebody with many talents that can create whatever reality I choose. I am powerful, I am smart, I will leave my mark in this world. No weapon formed against me shall ever prosper. I am worthy of all good things life has to offer. I am wealthy both in current And in spirit. I am healthy. I am wise, I am powerful, and I am great. Everybody has suffered from pain and depression in life. I promise you that life will get better. Stay strong keep your head up. Try to find your purpose with your life. Try to do something that makes you happy. Don't rely on someone to makes you happy. You have to find happiness in yourself and be around happy people. I am powerful. I am fearless. I am focused. I am a champion. Fill it! Believe it! All said I am the greatest if you realize how powerful your thoughts are you would never think a negative thought again!

Head Shepherd
P.O.G.
Loving Ministry

Spirit
I AM

Genesis 35:11 Then God said to him, I am the sovereign God. Be fruitful and multiply! A nation even a company of nations-will descend from you: kings will be among your descendants!

I am someone of importance that is worth more than gold. I am created in the image of god and do all things through him. He created the deep blue ocean, and a sunrise and set. I am one of those creations so, I can do or be anything if I just believe in him and myself. I am the child of the most high. I am a winner not a loser, I will defeat the enemy and worry no more about sorrow or pain I am a king or queen of my domain. I will not let no words of negativity put me down. I shall stay on the road of victory. I am a fighter and a survivor I will not be knocked down. My heavenly father has promised me that no weapon formed against me shall prosper. I am strong and mighty so no one will hold me down. I will trust in him and love everyone I am who god says I am. I will pray every day so the enemy will stay away. I will stay on the path of righteousness and not stray. I am worthy of praise and blessings each and every day. I will teach others to follow his words and be a light of hope. I am somebody who you can trust and lean on. I am a provider to the needy who needed the most. I am the head and not the tail. I will not fail in life. God says he is the beginning and the end. I am the alpha and the omega.

Head shepherd
POG

Spirit

I THINK

1 Corinthians 4:9 For I think, God has exhibited us apostles last of all, as men condemned to die, because we have become a spectacle to the world, both to angels and to people.

Good morning people of God. We as people of God are always saying I think I can or I think that it's right. Never knowing the true meaning of what we are saying. We are stopping ourselves from believing that we can do what we speak about and not willing to look up the answer to a question someone ask us. I think comes so easily for us to say not once putting any effort forth to believe we can achieve what we are saying. When you speak negative words over your life then your life will never be what you want it to be. Stop and think before you answer to a question being asked just make sure you know the answer. If not just say let me look up the answer. There is nothing wrong with looking up the answer it shows that you are a wise person. Remember if you want to be wise you must be around wise people. Please don't go around saying I think I have this sickness that is just the devil trying to keep you in his control. You should be using words of wholeness, good health speak these words over your life. Less turn I think into I know. Make sure you know what you are talking about when you talk to people about God or anything. Would you say I think I am going to heaven? You must know you are by following his words and laws then love people and have compassion for others in life. You must know what you want to do in life. Have some kind of plan in place to achieve what you want out of life. I think will never get you what you want in life you must know and believe in the things you want in life. God knows what you need and he will always provide you with what you need in life. Just know his laws and read his word and ask him to come in to your life. Then he can guide you through all the troubles life may bring your way. I THINK I CAN NO I KNOW I CAN!!

Head Shepherd
P.O.G.

Spirit
I WILL TRY

Job 34:9 For he says "There is no profit in trying to please God.

Good morning people of God. Why in life so many people are afraid to commit to something totally? We are always saying I will try to do it. Those are words of a quitter. If you want to be successful in anything in life you must be all in. Your mind set must be right believe you will achieve anything with the right thoughts. It may be difficult in the beginning just focus and don't give up. Have people around you that believe in your dream. Speak words of victory over your life. Stay positive and filled with hope knowing that this too shall come to pass. I will try to say no more, instead say I will I must make this happen. Ask your heavenly father for strength to complete this task. Pray daily first thing in the morning before walking out the door. You will and you can do all things through Christ. Know in your mind you are able to accomplish anything in life when you believe. People are satisfied with life eventually have even more reasons to be satisfied, because happiness leads to desirable outcomes school, and work, to fulfilling social relationships, and even to good health, and long life. There are always ways we can take control of a situation. Even when we initially believe we cannot. This is an area in which our minds way of responding to failure, and setback. Is misleading, and potentially damaging. We have to override the defeatism we feel, and find ways to assess control. That alone will help us move forward.

Head Shepherd
P.O.G
Loving Ministry

Spirit

I'M GONNA

Psalm 34:8 O taste and see that the lord is good: blessed is the man that trusteth in him.

Good morning people of God. P.O.G. remember when you were fresh out of high school? You wanted to rule the world. You was going to make all your dreams come true. Whatever your heart desired you were going to have. You was filled with energy, and passion for life. Your mind was filled with all types of new ideas you wanted to do in life. You were so ambitious you felt that the world was yours. Life is filled with unknowns, sickness, lost of job, kids, there are so many things that will put you off of your course. The next thing you know years has pass then decades. Whatever ever happened to the bight eyes and bushy tail person? Life has ways to put your dreams on the back burner. You must never stop believing in yourself or God. Keep hope alive your faith is stronger then man problems. Start believing again knowing that God will make away for your dreams. Start saying I'm going again then follow through with it. You can, you will when you have the almighty God on your side. There is nothing that you can do in life when he is backing you. All things become possible again. This is a new beginning so rise, and start living again. Life has so much to offer you there is so much you can do. Just have faith, and confidence in you. Your a warrior for Christ the devil cannot stop you. Take charge of your life.

Head Shepherd
P.O.G.
Loving Ministry

Spirit
IMPACTFUL LIFE

It's something I ask myself everyday. How can I have an impactful life? Am I living an impactful life? What is an impactful life? What is life all about? Am I living up to my expectations? There is so much to life than stuff. For many you reach a certain age, and seek the find the meaning of your life, and may even experience an emptiness. The secret of getting ahead is getting started. You can get everything in life you want if you just help enough other people get what they want. I can't change the direction of the wind, but I can adjust the sails to always reach my destination. Don't be afraid of failure because, it is necessary part of the journey. Embrace failure as a learning opportunity, and use it as a stepping stone to reach your next goal. In order to actually make the impact you want you must know exactly what behavior you want to have changed. You must think from why someone is doing what they are currently doing. When you have that information ask yourself what will motivate them to change. Look for potential pain points, and potential advantages. You need to speak to both sides. Then have a conversation, and in the conversation be open, be curious, be willing to really listen keep creating with the person you are wanting to impact.

Head Shepherd
P.O.G.
Loving Ministry

Spirit
I AM GOING TO TRY

Isaiah 29:15 Those who try to hide their plans from the Lord are as good as dead, who do their work in secret and boast, " Who sees us? Who knows what we're doing?

Good morning people of God. We as people of God are always stopping ourselves from succeeding in life with our words. When you speak negative words over your life nothing will turn out right in your life. God says to speak words of encouragement over your life. I am going to try is just a noble way of saying I am not going to make this happen for me. Your mind is like a computer what you think is what you will do. God says what a person think then that is what they are. I am going to try is always what a person says when they are not sure they can do something. The first thought that should be in your mind is I will overcome this and be great at doing this. I am going to try is for people who aren't sure of their Gods power. God says you can do all things through Christ if you just believe in him. With strong faith you can tell a mountain to move and it will. Positive thoughts can heal the sick and make the lame walk again. I am going to try "No" try and do it with all your thoughts on God letting you be a overcomer. Words have power if you just believe in them and have confidence in what you are saying. Change your words and change your life. Speak with authority knowing this shell happen for you. It is not ok because you tried trying to be better and being better are two very different things, and if we say, that it's ok for us to be the way we are, we accept the status quo of life. It is never ok to give up. It is never ok to use our weakness as an excuse to not try as hard as the rest of the People of God. We should be better than the world because we have gifts and talents from God and the world doesn't have that, Society can benefit from, and it is our responsibility to help people like no one ever help us. Be the better person, not the lesser one. If you have a problem fix it. I am going to try saying no more. Keep words of victory in your mind. Always pushing forward to win for Christ. People of God this isn't hard to do. If you just let him guide you through life. Faith is believing in the UN known, we go out each and every day not knowing what will happen to us. But that is faith. God is there to protect you from harm. I am going to try is another tool from the devil to keep you from God's mercy and grace. Whatever you want in life you must do it with God in it. He has promised you will achieve if you believe these are his words. Just try and see your life turn around to something good. Love yourself and others like Jesus and whatever you try in life will come to pass.

Head Shepherd
P.O.G.

Spirit

INSIGHT

The capacity to gain an accurate and deep intuitive understanding of a person or thing. We P.O.G. need to help those around us move forward to them find answers to the seemingly endless problems in politics, work, relationships and life. A new way of viewing the world that causes us to reexamine exiting conventions and challenge the status quo. Insight is not something you're just born with, it's something you learn. it's a perspective you can learn to take and a posture you can learn to exercise. Insightful people aren't necessarily the smartest people in the room, they've just put in the work of turning on their brain and exercising it regularly. Reading is to the mind what exercise is to the body. In a world full of people who waste their brains potential, the person who needs has taken a giant intellectual leap forward, But make sure you read widely become curious about divergent topics. Devour a book about the history of desert dwelling people while reading a novel, and working your way through a study about the psychological effects of solitary confinement on prisoners. Read frequently. Make it a habit. Trade Netflix for a book in bed and you'll be that much closer to being the most insightful person in the room. The future is completely open, and we are writing it moment to moment. It's not that some people have will power and some don't it's that some people are ready to change and others are not.

Head Shepherd
P.O.G.
Loving Ministry

Spirit
INSTINCTS

Jude 1:19 These are the people who divides you, who follow mere natural instincts and do not have the Spirit.

Have you ever felt that you know what we should be doing in life it seems like someone was telling you to go in this direction. Have you ever had something happened naturally without you even thinking about it? God has given you the ability to have control over your life. You are able to manifest whatever reality that you choose. You must learn to listen to that little voice in your head. That Is God talking to you. Your instinct is a connection to the universe. When we are able to step out on faith, and just go for it that is our true power. Life is filled with risk it comes a time when you must take the some. Have you ever heard the expression I can feel it in my gut? That is your body telling you to go for it! Stop thinking there will be a better time. Live in the moment and seize the opportunity. You are a creator in vision your possibility. Thoughts of greatness is the way to your future. Stop thinking little and start magnifying your God. When your able to think outside the box. You are building your reality. Your failures does not define you determination does. Work hard to achieve your dream stay consistent in life. Stay focus to accomplish what God has a in store for you. Become that person god created you to be in life. Have the future you always wanted. Nothing is more important than believing in yourself. Don't let the enemy stop you from moving forward. Keep going no matter what! Be brave stop letting fear make you not pursue your purpose. Never settle for less you deserve more in life. Your instincts know what you must do in life to have what you want. Never give up on it keep moving on to have it. God has one purpose for you let your instincts guide you. When we are able to let go and follow our heart. That is when we allow God in our lives.

Head Shepherd
P.O.G.
Loving Ministry

Spirit
INTENTION

James 1:25 But whoever looks intently into the perfect law that gives freedom, and continue in it not forgetting what they have heard, but doing it-they will be blessed in what they do.

Good morning my P.O.G. family. It time to stop the procrastination! Have some conviction for what is right in life that is Christ. Stop sitting on the fence, and get in the fight. This is no common enemy it is wickedness in high places. They disguised themselves behind those you trust. Don't believe everything you hear. Be informed, and research it for yourself. This world is slowly conforming so that the enemy can rule. We need God fearing people so that we can drive him back. All those who believe in a higher creator needs to wake up, and see whats really going on. There are systems being put in place to divide the people rich or poor. There is no more black or white. It's just one color the almighty green. Money will be the new ruler of this world. Believe us we need you to make a stand, and come together as one. I am asking all denomination that believe that compassion comes first, and not greed. To come together and speak out about all the injustices in the world. It's time to put aside all our petty differences, and stand as one. Man has been in charge for centuries all we got is much corruption. He comes just to rob, kill, and destroy the world. Its time we put God back into control so we can make this world what it is meant to be, and that's a planet of love. God is waiting on us to ask him. He will not let no harm come to his people. It's time for all believers to have strong faith in God again.

Head Shepherd
P.O.G.
Loving MInistry

Spirit

INTUITION

God has given you a sense of knowing what's right or wrong in your life. Your health should tell you when you're doing wrong. the ability to understand something immediately without the need for conscious reasoning. We live in a fear-based culture that obsesses on trying to control life. We're terrified of uncertainty. So we're constantly anticipating everything that might go wrong, and doing everything within our power to guide, or guard against inevitable disaster. It's an exhausting way to live, and it can lead to a chronic state of stress, anxiety, and exhaustion. You don't need fear to protect you, because you have intuition. We are all equipped with an intuition that is a potent, trustworthy, and impeccably attain to our true path. In order to make our best decision, we need a balance of intuition which serves to bridge the gap between instinct, and reasoning irrational thinking. A sensing person will look at the details of the situation. They will use their senses to examine the evidence, and hand and intuitive person will think More abstractly about information. They will Focus on future possibilities, and patterns. Sometimes your own intuition can tell you more than 7 watchmen on a high tower. develop an intuition requires cultivate an awareness, slowing down, and listening to your inner voice. pay attention to your body's reaction and notice. When you're good is telling you something important. Practice meditation or mindfulness to quiet your mind, and enhance your ability to tune into your intuition. Trust yourself and don't second, guess your intuition. with practice, you'll become more confident in your ability to make into intuitive decisions and trust guidance that comes from within. Remember intuition as a skill that can be developed with time and patience.

Head Shepherd
P.O.G.
Loving Ministry

Spirit

INVALUABLE

....

Do you have that one person who everyone turns to? For advice, answers, guidance, or even a smile on a rainy day? They are usually cheerful without being annoying and somehow always available in spite of the calendar. Far more full than yours or mine. To you to me and to everyone else they touches, they are invaluable. You must be one of those people who was born with the right mix of charm and grace right? Invaluable people have learned and externalized a few key qualities that anyone can master. A perfect mix of charm, and grace is not what makes people invaluable. Empathy, pro activity, and an attitude of gratitude is what will make the person no one can let go. 'Believe you can and you're halfway there. People of God, we needed to be people of love and want to uplift others. Listen to people give them advice that will help them. Giving is one of the things people will never forget about you doing for them. You will never be happy if you continue to search for what happiness consists of, you will never live if you are looking for the meaning of life. The only limits you have are the limits you set for yourself. Push beyond your comfort zone, embrace challenges, and let your determination fuel your success. You have what it takes to conquer anything. Be a people person who live there life to serve others, be invaluable to all creations!

Head Shepherd
P.O.G.
Loving Ministry

Spirit
IT'S IN YOU!

When will we as people of God start living up to our true potential? The universal God has placed Limitless possibilities in you. All you have to do is just believe. You are able to create whatever environment you choose to live in life. No matter what the circumstance may be. You are able to choose the emotions you focus on good, or sad. You have the ability to decide how you're going to live life. Stop letting others tell you how to live your life. Take back the authority over it yourself. There is nothing you cannot do or nothing you can not have when you have choose to. We as Believers are all positive energy. That connect us to the universal God. We all have the same DNA as the universal God. That mean that there is something special within you. We're all made of energy being positive or negative. Imagine if we were all on the same frequency of positivity. What an environment we could create. of vibration, of loving peace, happiness, and a goodwill to all humanity. There will be no more sorrow or pain to afflict us. This world would be a beautiful place, because God will be within us. It's real simple is all about your perception of Life stop letting the enemy divide us. With all of his manipulating devices. You have been given free will so choose to live in harmony with each other. Why not have a protest of love, and sit down, and talk about our differences and not yell at each other. We are only using 1% of our own mind. Imagine if we use the other 99% you are a powerful spirit.

Head Shepherd
P.O.G.
Loving Ministry

Spirit
I GUESS

....

1 Timothy 6:17 command those who are rich in this world's goods not to be haughty or to set their hope on riches, which are uncertain, but on God who richly provides us with all things for our enjoyment.

Good morning people of God. People of God we must stop saying I guess when you are not sure about something. We must know gods commandments and laws. So we can tell others with confidence. God's people are not unsure about life we know what is expected of us. I guess is a weak minded saying. Have confidence in the words you speak out of your mouth. We are children of Christ we know what is expected of us in life. If you want anything positive to happened to you then think about it, then speak about it. Others are watching us to see if we are living his commandments. Say I guess no more. Change it to I know with a voice of certainty. Have faith and believe in yourself you can change the course of your life with your words. You must know where you want to be in life. I guess things will turn out alright. No change your mind and words. Then you will know that things will turn out right in your life. When you have positive thoughts then positive things will happen for you. God says a person is who they think they are have a good outlook for your life. Doubt about when to have the serenity to accept or the courage to try to change things, about when to care and when to not care, about when to try harder, and when to give up, about when to keep doing what you're doing, and when to do something else, about when to hold out for delayed uncertain gratification, and when to hold on to that bird in the hand rather than trying for those two in the bush. Even doubt about when to second guess yourself and when to shut up, and just keep at whatever you are doing.

There's a thin line between situations that call for one or the other of these opposed options study it. We as people of God must not guess we must know the basic instruction before leaving earth just read this book and it will prepare you to meet your heavenly father.

Head Shepherd
P.O.G.
Loving Ministry

Spirit
IT'S YOU

There comes a time in life when you have to be you. No matter what other people will think of you. We all want to be someone of importance in life. Time pass so quickly so you need to make every moment count. Don't wait till the end of your life to be who you were created to be. To become the best version of your self you have to know your purpose. Think what do you want to become best at. Being the best doesn't have to be about fame or power. Fear of failure is a mental, emotional, awareness that success may not be possible. To much fear and failure can hinder success and accomplishment while too little fear of failure may not motivate you enough. Here's the thing fear get your full attention. When you are running from a pack of wild dogs you will be 100 percent present in the moment. And goals that are not frightening are not worth having. Think about your goals and dreams. Are they big enough. What are the chances you will achieve them? Do you have the emotional intelligence required to embrace fear, and move forward? Things may come to those who wait, but only the things left by those who hustle. I'm a big believer in evolution, growth, and in being the best you that you can be, and I feel like the first step to doing that is mentally healthy. What helps you preserver is your resilience, and commitment. Don't limit yourself. Many people limit themselves to what they think they can do. You can go as far as your mindset let's you. What you believe remember you can achieve.

Head Shepherd
P.O.G.
Loving Ministry

Spirit
JOY

Everything in life is easier when you don't concern yourself with what other people are saying. It is better to light a candle than to complain about the darkness. Be the change that you wish to see in the world. Sometimes the road of life is a bumpy one if you want to master joyful living. Be open to learning from the challenges that life brings you. Be honest about what buttons get pushed, and recognize when you have a drop into a hole that you can't seem to find your way out of. No matter what is going on in your life show up in a good natured way. No one likes a negative person. Stop complaining instead, be patient, open, kind, agreeable in your day-to-day life. All you need to do is recognize what brings you joy then follow it. Make room in your life for what is positive, light, and life affirming being aside all the time keeps to low. Once you get outside however something immediately changes. But one thing you're breathing in more oxygen getting this life affirming element into your lungs, and doing something profoundly good for your body. There's always much to see outdoors, no matter the season time of day where you are geographically, and whether you're by yourself or with others. I love to walk in nature. It calms me helps me to focus relieve stress works up a sweat and makes me feel like I have given myself a gift when you're appreciative you're thankful for what you will receive, and demonstrate your appreciation and words and deeds. Then you will have joy in your life.

Head Shepherd
P.O.G
Loving Ministry

Spirit

KEEP YOUR ENERGY!

Colossians 1:29 To this end I strenuously contend with all the energy Christ so powerfully works in me.

The most precious thing that you have in life is your happiness. Be a good cheer and appreciate your life. The most important thing you can have in life is your energy. Is what keep you moving throughout your reality. The feeling of being filled with positive energy is amazing. There is no other feeling in the world when your living in your true purpose the energy inside of you is really high. There isn't nothing you feel you can not do. Be willing to try something you thought you could not do with positive thought you will achieve all things. When we are able to be filled with the positive energy that is when life really means something. You have control over your life with your thoughts you can make it go in any direction that you choose. Just be field with the Holy Spirit knowing God is working through you. All things become possible with god's energy is working through you. Your frequency of the universe must be high to connect you to him. When we are on a level of high energy. That is when we can create a new world. A world of happiness peace & love for all our true power is love and empathy for one another. Joy in our heart will always keep us healthy. P.O.G it is time we realize that Christ is the only way to everlasting life. We are here to show all that Jesus will fix it no matter what the enemy is trying to do in your life.

Head Shepherd
P.O.G.
Loving Ministry

Spirit

KNOWING YOUR WORTH

Everyone wants to contribute to destiny but nobody wants to be committed. Do the different things while they are easy, and do the great things while they are small. A journey of a A 1000 miles Must begin with a single step. He whom says he can, and he who says he cannot are both usually right. There are so many words to describe how we feel about ourselves. how we think about ourselves, and how we get toward ourselves. It's understandable if they all start to blend together for you. However they are indeed different concepts with unique meanings, findings and purposes. It's not necessary to have a high sense of self confidence in every area of your life. There are naturally some things that you will simply not be very good at, and other areas in which you will excel. The important thing is to have self confidence in the activities in your life that matter to you. In a high sense of self worth overall. Self worth is at the core of our very selves, our thoughts, feelings, and behaviors, are intimately tied into how we view our worthiness, and value as human beings. There are things you can do to boost your sense of self worth, and ensure that you value yourself like you ought to be valued as a full complete, and wonderful human being that is deserving of love, and respect, no matter what. Create the person you want to be. Build the life you want to live dream what you want to see come to reality you have what it take!

Head Shepherd
P.O.G.
Loving Ministry

Spirit
KEEPING YOUR WORD

Your words have power, so speak words of encouragement, victory, and positivity. Speak life into others let them know that they matter. Be that cheer leader in life! Live each and every day with energy to brighten up someone's life. Believe you can, And you're halfway there. When you tell someone you're going to do something for them, keep your word people should not have to figure you out. Be that person of excellence always telling the truth, don't let others opinions define who you are!

In life, people will always have problems be that coach to help them figure them out. You're only as good as your word. In a world where politicians, notably and consistently don't keep their word. It is easy for the general public to do them saying. After all, politicians are often viewed as leaders and moral beacons, so their behavior can become normalized, in the public eye. In reality, political issues often aren't moral authorities, and in my opinion, should be personalized each time. They break their word for breaking their constituents trust. Where is the type of accountability in our society today? Why do we accept people breaking their word as normal. Words have power, so use them to empower others. Keeping your word is about more than just doing what you say. You will, it is about showing you have someone's back. It doesn't matter if the task is menial. If you say you will get it done. Do it because that builds credibility, trust and self accountability.

Head Shepherd
P.O.G.
Loving Ministry

Spirit
KNOWING WHO YOU ARE

Determination becomes obsession, and then it becomes all that matter. To truly know yourself you must know how you would react in any situation emotionally your mind, and spirit must become as one we humans are a funny lot to say the lease. We know so much in so many areas of life that it is unnecessary to mention the high points. Yet for all our spectacular accomplishments our basic human nature which is at the core of our existence, and the source of our experience in this world, seems to remain a mystery for most of us. You must first know yourself To be curious about that which is not my concern, while I am still ignorant of my own self would be ridiculous. I have to believe that we are all somewhat guilty of this. As a collective whole, and we are so knowledgeable of our pop culture, celebrities, and sports. This makes for nice casual conversation, but does little to improve the true quality of our lives. The foundation of our self image, and are self esteem are not strengthened by superficial trivial pursuits knowing yourself can surely help with some of the confusion, and conflict and life. If we can understand How we react to life with our instructional strength, and our weaknesses we can gain more control over our actions, and make better choices. I rather someone hate me, and get better than like me, and stay the same. Whatever you focus on determines what you get from life. If the enemy within you is defeated the enemy outside you can do no harm.

Haed Shepherd
P.O.G.
Loving Ministry

Spirit
KNOW

Psalms 119:68 The lord is good to all and his tender mercies are all over his works.

G ood morning people of God. Do you know what you want out of life? What you really want to do with your life? Are you just living day by day not knowing what you want to do with your life? There is something great inside of you just waiting to get out and show off. God has placed greatness in you believe this his words are true. Take inventory of your life,and find out what you are passionate about in life. There is something that you do better than anyone else find out what that is. Then do it over and over again until you have perfected it. Know you are a child of God made in his image. The world has so much to offer you just know what you are capable of doing. There would be no stopping you when you have God on your side. Remember there are those who do not want you to know what they know. They need to feel that they are better than you by knowing more than you. Some will not be as uplifting as others in life. Make sure you have people on your side who will encouraged you to know all you can know about life. Just have faith knowing God is there with you along this journey. Your mind is the most powerful thing you have working for you. Imagine what you want in life, and believe this will happen for you. Know that you are able to have your dreams.

Head Shepherd
P.O.G.
Loving Ministry

Spirit
KNOCK DOWN

Psalms 36:12 I can see the evil doers! They have fallen they have been knocked down and are unable to get up!

Good morning people of God we as people of God must stop letting the devil knock us down in life. Some of us when we are knocked down we stay down. Not wanting to believe in the heavenly father anymore. There is a three count in boxing you must get up before the count of three. I know that this is a hard knocked life, but we must be warriors for Christ the ups and downs of life is part of what you must go through. Those are the times when God is getting you ready for the fight of your life. The devil will do and say anything to keep you down in life. You must be stronger and filled with faith to get up and go on. There are so many hard blows in life you must take them. This is the times you must believe that this won't keep you down. Unemployment, sickness, and death, those are the times when you are rocked the hardiest in life. Your legs buckle and you see stars. You don't know where your next breathe will come from. But I am here to tell you to hold on change is coming. These are the times when Jesus will carry you through the troubles of life. God says I will be your strength when you are weak just believe in me and you shall grow strong. Just have a positive mind set and believe in him. Say to yourself I am a child of God. This shall not keep me down. Devil loose me you have no authority over me. I'm a fighter, a warrior for god. I know in my times when I cannot do it in my own strength my heavenly father will do it in his. So Satan get back jack. I am going to get up and be a winner again. For I know that there is no weapon formed against me shall prosper. We are P.O.G. this means we are winners in life.

Head Shepherd
P.O.G.

Spirit
LAUGH

....

Our mouths were filled with laughter our tongue with song of joy. Then it was said among the nation the Lord has done Great things for them. Psalm 126:2 when you are able to laugh at yourself it means you are not frustrated with your life. Laughter is the medicine for the soul. It makes you feel warm all over. Whenever the pressure of life gets to you just laugh out loud. It will calm the soul. Its true laughter is strong medicine. It draws people together in ways that trigger healthy physical, and emotional change in the body. Laughter strengthens your immune system, boost mood, diminish pain, and protects you from the damaging effects of stress. Nothing works better too bring your mind and body back into balance then a good laugh. Laughter is an amazing ability that God gave us all. Laughter helps us cope with sadness, and life. We live in a falling world of pain. It's sometimes hard to laugh. It's difficult to read the news on a daily basis, and not feel the inward groaning of the spirit at the hardship of this world. Yet though the Holy Spirit we can experience a taste of heaven with a sincere, and pure joy. What we must remember is no matter how dark the times may seem Jesus will never leave you he will never forsake you. He has plans to prosper you and not hurt you. Trust him because he truly loves you. Sometimes God have us go through things in life just so we can be a helped to others.

Head Shepherd
P.O.G.
Loving Ministry

Spirit LAWS

Isaiah 55:9 For as the heavens are higher than the earth, so are my ways higher than your ways, and my thoughts than your thoughts.

Good morning people of God. Most people in society today have no problem following the authority laws. Even if they are right or wrong we just follow them. The government today are so busy passing all types of laws. Saying it is for the betterment of men. There once was a law on the books stating that women cannot vote. Be careful who you follow. When you follow Gods laws you know its the right thing to do. God laws are for the people rich or poor. He loves you unconditionally. The laws of the father are put into place so you can live more abundantly. God laws are for the people of god to keep them from harm.

When you follow his laws your life will always turn out right. When you are obedient to him you will always have what is good in life. Just pray for consistency to follow his laws. Man laws are designed to protect those who are empowered. Educate yourself, and know the laws of the land. If you study them you will see they are not designed for the least of thee. Your heavenly father laws were always protect you from mans.

Head Shepherd
P.O.G.
Loving Ministry

Spirit
LIGHT OF HOPE

1 Chronicles 29:15 We are foreigners and strangers in your sight, as were all our ancestors. Our days on earth are like a shadow, with out hope.

Good morning my P.O.G. family. I know in these uncertain times there is a lot of worry and fear going on. God has not given up on us yet! In every situation in life we must learn to see the good in it. The doctors, the first res ponders are putting themselves in harms way to take care of us. Parents are teaching their children about God, and spending some valuable time together. People are eating more healthy, and working out at home again. We are beginning to learn why God put us here that is to have compassion, and love for one another again. This is a global thing we must learn to replace the hate in our hearts with love. God so loved the world there is nothing he will not do to keep you away from harm. He just ask you to believe in the son, spirit, and the father. Even though there is so much uncertainty all around us just look at the season it is still going on. The grass is green the flowers are in bloom, and the trees' are beginning to bud. God is not a destroyer of life. God created the birds, and the bee's and the air that you breathe. He is a just God trying to tell you that he is in control. He knows what the enemy is up to. He is trying to protect you. Just fall on your knees, and give him praise. He is going to get your through the uncertainties of life. Have faith these are the times of the true believers that knows that God is still on the thrown. God will deliver you from all your frustrations in life, and put joy back into your heart again.

Head Shepherd
P.O.G.
Loving Ministry

Spirit
LIFE

Don't over blame yourself for the problems in your life. Accept things and go forward. Don't let others define who you are. Get up and learn the skills needed, and go after it all the keys to a happy life is in your hands. Remember the moment you accept total responsibility for everything in your life is the moment you align the power to change anything in your life. God has a plan for each of us. He created this earth, and sent us here so we could have faith, and find joy. Our challenges help us grow, and prepare us to live with one another. God made it pretty clear that families, and friends are important. Families are central to God's plan for his children. They are the fundamental building block of strong societies. Families are where we can feel love, and learn how to love others. Life is tough, and we need people we can lean on. Home is a safe haven where we can get love, advice, and support. Our family here on Earth is organized like our family in heaven. Much like we can go to our parents for advice our heavenly father is always there to give us help. When we pray he listens and answer. God loves us so much. He loves us even when we make mistakes. Matthews 21:22 and all thing whatever. Ye shall ask in prayer believing ye shall receive.

Head Shepherd
P.O.G.
Loving Ministry

Spirit
LIFE

John 1:4 In him was life, and that life was the light of all mankind.

We spend our whole lives waiting on the right moment, to enjoy our lives. Never once living in that moment of the now. You are not promised tomorrow, so enjoy them now. This world has changed so dramatically. You do not know what tomorrow will bring. Live in the now being grateful, and thankful for the people in your life. The most precious thing on this Earth is loving between one another. Stop seeking materialistic things in life. Those things can be easily taken away. When you have someone you love, and they love you back. That is truly living life! The essence of life is joy, and happiness about the world which you live in. Your heavenly father loves you with all his heart. He just want you to just love back. When you start living your life with your heart things would not be so difficult. You are truly living when you don't let fear dictate your life. When you stand firm, on God's words the enemy has no authority over you. We have been given dominion over this land. When we start living to help one another, and not seeking money, and control of others. Then this world will be a wonderful place filled with love. The enemy has deceived us to believe to live for money, and not for love. The way it's supposed to be. It's time to change this mindset, and start living for one another too beautify this world again. It's time to stop living your life in fear, and anxiety. God did not give you that type of spirit. He gave you a spirit of love and happiness. God has placed a guardian angel around you to protect you. Just listen and they will guide you through life troubles.

Head Shepherd
P.O.G.
Loving Ministry

Spirit LIFTING

The best thing you can do for someone in life is to lift their spirits about life. God has placed in our hearts the desire to love each other stop being so judgmental towards everyone in life. Let down the wall around your heart, and let God in to guide you.. We all need someone to open up and talk about the problems in life. This enemy has made this world so crazy. People don't want to be around one another. We are social able people we need each other. Be willing to encourage and inspire everyone. This universe is like a magnet whatever you put out there will always come back to you John 6:33 I have told you these things so that in me you may have peace. In this world you will have trouble. But take heart! I have overcome the world we all need one another kindness, to be able to get through the storms In life. A kind word helps people cope with the difficulty in life be willing to have a positive word to say about others. There are 2 forces in you positive, and negative force.. They are both equal however, for you to be normal one of them must rise above the other. You have to inspire people by changing the way they think and feel about themselves so that they want so to take positive action. Your behavior will inspire people more than anything else. The only way to call the best out of others is to expect the best from yourself.

Head Shepherd
P.O.G.
Loving Ministry

Spirit
LIGHT

We are the light of the world. You have a responsibility of being the light of hope for others. Personal growth is not a matter of learning new information but unlearning old limits. Most great accomplishments were achieved by the people who at 1st had no idea what they were doing. One of the remarkable things about life today is the fact that science knows so much about some things, and so little about some other things which are very common, and we intend to take those things for granted not sensing how very important they are to our survival. Light conveys both an absence of darkness, and equality that will help us to see, and understand more clearly. The light of wisdom will guide us through troubled times, and challenges how often do we seek a wise person's council when we are feeling stuck with an issue, in a relationship, or at work. Light also communicates levity or joy. A light heart is wise not held down by heavy emotions, and thoughts of doom or despondency the person who is light in nature lasts easily, and takes life as it comes. A blessing of light at any time is a great gift to give or receive.

Head Shepherd
P.O.G.
Loving Ministry

Spirit

LIP SERVICE

Leviticus 5:4 Or if a soul swear, pronouncing with his lips to do evil, or to do good, whatsoever it be that a man shall pronounce with an oath, and it be hid from him: when he knoweth of it, then he shall be guilty in one of these.

Good morning people of god. We as people of god must watch out for people who are trying to tell us what we want to hear. There are politicians and doctors, lawyers, who think that they have the answers for everything that is wrong in life. My mother once said you have to watch out for those silver tongue devils. Just wanting to lead you down the road of destruction. We are so willing to let anyone tell us what we want to hear, and we will buy into it very easily. When something sounds to good to be true most of the time it is . Listen to that voice in your head that is telling you don't do it. If you ask God for guidance and he tells you what to do and there is no sin in it then do it. People are so willing to tell us something just so they can have their way with us. If there is no sin in any decision you make then go ahead with it. If you are unsure of something then ask questions because the devil don't like to explain himself. Some of us are so worried about life that we will listen to anyone who sounds like they know what is right in life. Remember man is only concerned about himself trying to take advantage of you or what you have. Lip service can also come from your love ones too. Be careful who you listen to in life, what SEEMS GOOD AT FIRST is not .and what seems to be justice is not really justice at all. We should be listening to gods words and do as he asked then there will be no need to worry about are we doing what is right. Trust in him and his son to lead you down the path of righteousness pray for guidance, and help in any life decision you may have. It will always turn out right.

Head Shepherd
POG

Spirit
LOVE

Be positive. Your mind is more powerful than you think. What is down in the well comes up in the bucket. Feel yourself with love. Whatever your mind think it will see if you want to see the positive in life starting thinking, and looking at the positive in life. Love is such a powerful force. Is there for everyone to embrace that kind of unconditional love for all of the humankind. That is the kind of love that impel people to go into the community, and try to change conditions for others, to take risks for what they believe in. Teach your body emotionally what it would feel to believe In this way to be empowered to be moved by your own greatness, to be invincible to be in love with life to feel unlimited, and to live as if your prayers are already answered. Never look to others for what your own sense of self worth, self esteem, self belief, or self love as the answers ultimately must come from yourself. Self love does not mean you're selfish it means that you're finally learned what makes you happy what your standards, and boundaries are. When you have love present in your mind, heart, and spirit. There is no darkness that can consume you, because love is the light of the way. Love is a universal emotion. That is what connects us all to each other. Corinthians chapter 13 verse 2 if I have the gift of prophecy and can Phantom all mysteries and all knowledge and if I have a faith that can move mountains but do not have love I am nothing.

Head Shepherd
P.O.G
Loving Ministry

Spirit LEADERS

Timothy 5:17 Elders who provide effective leadership must be counted worthy of double honor, especially those who work hard in speaking and teaching.

Good morning people of God. God has placed a leadership role in all of us. We do his will each and every day not knowing others are watching us. God must always show in whatever you are doing in life. People of God are people who lead others into the light of Jesus Christ. Leaders are made by the word of Christ and his laws. We are called as leaders to serve others, and never stop loving God and others. A good leader always put others needs above their own. We must make sure Gods people are well taken care of, and then you will also be taken good care of by God. A leader does not have to be in a high position. We all have the capability to lead others to the path of righteousness. Read the bible it will tell and teach you how to be a great leader to others. As long as you have a caring heart you can be a leader. God even took Moses who couldn't speak without stuttering every other word out of his mouth and made him a great leader. He went to Faro and told him to let my people go from slavery. You don't have to be perfect to be a leader just caring about humanity. It is the jobs of leaders to develop a person establish what matters and articulate why set direction and inspire others. We all have the ability to provide, as spouses, and as friends. To find a reason to want to lead we only need to remember that when we provide leadership, we create value. And value creation creates happiness.

Head Shepherd
P.O.G.

Spirit

LOOKING FORWARD TOO

Genesis 49:18 I wait for your deliverance O Lord.

Good morning people of God. We as P.O.G. are always looking forward to the good things in life. We work all week long looking forward to the weekend. Then we work all year long looking forward to a vacation. Students spend years in school looking forward to graduate. We all want something to make us happy in life. We need to have a attitude of gratefulness and just be happy where we are at. Positive thinking will always keep you in a great mood. Look at life differently see the joy in it. Believe in something wonderful like love and happiness. Being upset all the time will not make you appreciate the beauty in life. When you have a peaceful heart and mind you are calmer. When you are at a relax state you are able to think more clearly. When there are no unclean thoughts on your mind, then God is ready to listen to you. Ask him what is the meaning of life? When he tells you just do as he told you. Be that person of loving, caring and sharing with others. Then you can look forward to a much more enjoyable life. When you start living for Christ you start living new again meaning that all your sins has been forgiven you are a new creature. Just keep love and happiness in your heart all the time. God will always keep the devil far away from you as long as you pray for him to help you. Everyday will become something to look forward to now that God is in your life. You should be looking forward to the day you meet your heavenly father. Start now preparing yourself for that day. Cleanse yourself of all sins and be a good servant to others. Love yourself and then you will be able to love others. Have a heart of compassion when you see and hear about all the wrong in life. Be like Jesus and show your father you are worthy of his praise. So on that day you meet your heavenly father he will say "job well done my faithful servant". Wouldn't that be something really to look forward too?

Head Shepherd
P.O.G.
Loving Ministry

Spirit
LOOKING FORWARD TOO

Job35:14 how much less then, when you say that you do not perceive him, that the case is before him and you are waiting for him!

Good morning people of God. People in life always want something they can look forward to, so they can enjoy. We work all week long just looking forward to the weekend. Students spend years in school looking forward to graduations. Ladies are looking forward to the day they will get married. We all want something that can make us happy in life. True happiness lives within you. God has given you the ability to control your thoughts with your mind. Whatever you're thinking about will always put you in a certain mood. You have to have some belief within yourself. By knowing you can do this. Total control over your thoughts isn't a easy thing to do. Most people don't believe in themselves. To be able to make this happen. Good is what the heavenly father wants for us. There is bad all around us. So that is what we are always thinking about. Change the way you look at life, and be able to see the good of things in life. Looking forward to something wonderful can be everyday of your life. The power lives within you. Try and use your mind. You can't act in life without first anticipating what you are going to do. Being able to predict or anticipate the future enables us to prepare for it by taking the action we think are necessary to meet future event with success. We make predictions about what we are expecting in life based on our pass experience, and the things we've learned to believe are true. Our memory is what gives us the ability to store information about our pass experience, so that we can use it to anticipate what will happen in the future. In general, the ability to predict future experience based on we've learned is a very good thing that facilitates our ability to survive the world. If a person or situation we encounter seems dangerous in some way we can remember to avoid that person or place in the future. However if you have bad habits, self - destructions patterns, or simply a pass that you would like to break free from so that you can create a better life, this system can keep you trapped unknowingly. The important thing to recognize here is the past is only relevant to the extent that you use it to make future predictions. It is your thinking about the future and what you are expecting in life that leads to your actions that create the experience you end up living. The good news, is that once you are aware of it you can intercept this process, recognize the old beliefs, and begin to generate new expectations, and ways of thinking about your future, that will results that will, in different actions. We as people of god must always be looking forward to judgment day. The day when the lord will say you been a good servant and let you in to the kingdom of God. Oh happy days.

Head Shepherd
People of God
Loving Ministry

Spirit

MAKING SOMEONE'S DAY BETTER

Want to make someone's day? Spreading some warmth with random acts of kindness? You can show kindness to anyone anywhere, with anything as simple as a smile or a thank you. The more intimate the gesture the more intimate the relationship should be. If you strive to live an altruistic lifestyle there are lots of ways to serve others, and most of them don't have to be grandiose, or extravagant. They're simply conscious. Selfless decisions during day to day activities. Even a small gesture can have a huge influence, on the people around you. Being kind to yourself, and those around you might feel challenging. This difficulty may stem from personality traits, fears, about what others think of you low self-esteem or challenging circumstances. If you want to be kinder you might want to try making eye contact smiling using your conversation partners name, and being an active listener during interactions. Each person has a unique personality with positive, and negative, characteristics. You may have certain character qualities that others admire in, you like courage, tenacity, leadership, loyalty, and contentment. Try to credit yourself for the qualities you possess instead of those you might struggle with. You may find that some people think you're unkind while others find you gentle, kind, and empathetic, finding people you're compatible with may reduce the chances of feeling unkind if it is a matter of personality. believe in yourself, and unleash the unstoppable force within! You've got the power to change people to becoming better.

Head Shepherd
P.O.G.
Loving Ministry

Spirit

MANIFESTING

Ephesians 5:13 But everything exposed by light becomes visible- and everything that is illuminated becomes a light.

This is a World War 3 against Satan. It's a psychological War to control your mind, and your belief. This enemy wants us to live in fear, and anxiety, and negativity. He knows if he can do this he will possess us. God says You must keep guard over your mind. Watch what you believe what the media is telling you. The only way to defeat this enemy is to keep your joy, happiness, and positive attitude. With these emotions you have a formula for victory over the devil. This enemy wants to keep the vibrations of the world low. He knows we cannot survive with that type of energy. We need energy of positivity, and a frequency of the most high. Connecting us with the Divine Universal God. When we are connected with our creator the enemy knows he has no authority over us. The universal God will call out his armies. To keep the enemy from harming us and our loved ones. There comes a time when you have to stand up, and tell the Enemy No More. It is over you have no authority over my life. God has given me dominion over the land. I will live my life being fruitful, and multiplying sharing love to all of humanity. It's time to stop living in fear, and go out and enjoy your life again. God did not give you a spirit of fear. You must be able to bring this reality that you want in to existence by believing you can.

Head Shepherd
P.O.G.
Loving Ministry

Spirit
MEANINGFUL LIFE!

When you reach a point in life, to serve others you living a meaningful life. A meaningful life is one where you feel connected to the world around you in all aspects of your life. This can be a deep connection with nature or an emotional connection with another person. A meaningful life is one where you feel connected to the people and places you care about most. What we do, who we spend time with how we spend our leisure time, and where we choose to live all impact the kind of life we lead. That said, there is no one right way to live a meaningful life. Different people are inherently more prone to other interest, and habits based on their personalities. For the meaning of life differs from man to man, from day to day and from hour to hour. What matters therefore is not the meaning of life in general, but rather the specific meaning of a person's; life at a given moment. At some stage of our time on earth we might wonder about the meaning of our life. Our life circumstances and experiences change as we age. We go through various life stages, such as parenthood, and career changes, and each stage presents us with unique challenges and achievements. Keep in mind that the meaning of life is created by you. Experience things you've always wanted to try. And build a lasting connection to your community. Its all these thing that give our life meaning. When you reflect on your life in old age, you'll feel blessed with the things you've done if you chose to live life on your terms.

Head Shepherd
P.O.G.
Loving Ministry

Spirit MEDICINE

Proverbs 17:22 A cheerful heart is good medicine, but a crushed spirit dries up the bones.

Did you know that the hippocratics corpus is a collection of around seventy early medical works from ancient Greece strongly associated with Hippocrates and his students. Most famously The hippocratics invented the Hippocratic oath for physicians. We all in society are on some type of medication that our doctor has prescribe us. There are so many types of medication for whatever ales you. The world is filled with so much sickness, and disease it seems like everyone has something wrong with them. We depend on these pills to make us feel better. Not once thinking about what is it doing to us. There are so many side effects to these drugs from blindness to death. But yet we still take them with out no worries, because the doctor tells us to. Even Michael Jackson, and Prince died from something that was prescribe by a doctor. We need to call on a higher power to heal us, and that is Jesus. God has promise you that you can get healed in the name of Jesus. Your mind is a powerful thing believe in his words, Knowing that healing is on the way. Man medicine is only temporary, but Gods words are forever good. There is no sorrow or pain he cannot heal you of. He is the great physician he can do all things when you believe in him. Have faith know all things are possible in his words. Pray each, and every day of healing, and holiness is on the way. Believe this with all of your being. Then read the book of healing the bible each and every day.

Head Shepherd
P.O.G.
Loving Ministry

Spirit

MENTORING

Matthew 25:35 For I was hungry and you gave me something to eat, I was thirsty and you gave me something to drink, I was a stranger and you invited me in.

What is the meaning of life? We all was put here on this planet to teach others about Christ. When you are able to help others then your doing what is right. To show people how something is done means a lot more to than telling them. Most people learn better when they see others doing it. God said work without action is dead. Christ came to Earth to show us how to love. True love Is always unconditional. When someone love you you truly, they will never expect something back from you. Teaching is the greatest gift from God. You are developing someone's mind to do God's will. We have to mentor when they are small around the age of 6. Teach them to be someone that loves humanity. Show them by loving them unconditionally. In order to change the world we must change how we see the world. Let love guide you by showing others to live right. The greatest comment a person can give you is thank you for caring. When you are able to help others you will be tremendously empowered. We are all connected in life so we must be able to help each other through it. We are spiritual beings having a human experience together. Feeling abundant and grateful in knowing that we are here for each other. The answers are within us all. If we just take time to listen to each other then we will know exactly what needs to be done in life stay consistent, stay positive, and know you can make a difference in someone's life. I believe in humanity as a whole, all lives matter.

Head Shepherd
P.O.G.
Loving Ministry

Spirit MERRY!

> Proverbs 17:22 A cheerful heart is good medicine, but a crushed spirit dries up the bones.

This year has been so uncertain there has been so much going on in the world. This enemy is hard at work trying to steal our soul. When you let someone drain your energy its easy to control your perspective of life. We must stay focus on our own positive energy in our mind. You must believe all things are possible with Christ. God said I commend joy for men has nothing better under the Sun but to eat and drink and be joyful, for this will go with him in his toil through the days of his life that God has given him under the Sun. It's time to start enjoying our lives again and stop letting this evil keep us in fear. We need people of God to celebrate the wonders in our life. Live for the new beginnings knowing that this also shall pass. We are able to create whatever environment we choose to live in life. Your thoughts are your connection to the universal God. He has given you free will to choose how you would like to live. Love, hate or positive negative which emotion would you choose. Positive is to build-up in negative is to tear down. God wants us to beautify the world. Show kindness to one another and love everyone no matter what color. Tell yourself I am going to live life enjoying every moment I live in life. Smile be happy in every situation in your life Just know God want you to have every desire of your heart. With God we have a great future in stored for us. Time has come to stop living in fear, and step out on faith. To be who God created you to be someone who is loved. To change the quality of your life change the quality of your thinking.

Head Shepherd
P.O.G
Loving Ministry

Spirit
MIND

Ephesians 4:31-32 Let all bitterness and wrath and anger and clamor, and evil speaking be put away from you with all malice. And be ye kind to one another even as God for Christ's sake halt forgiven you.

Good Morning People of God. Anger is an evil spirit of the enemy he uses to hurt people. Just read your Bible and pray to God to take it away from your mind and soul. Anger can also be that somebody mistreated you, took advantage of you, you not liking yourself where you work at or hate the people around you.

In this situation, you have control of it. Just change what you don't like about yourself and where you work and the people you are with. People who hold onto anger often don't realize it, but they are poisoning their own lives. It doesn't make any sense to stay angry for what somebody has already done to you in the past. Let go of the hurts and pains. Start fresh again. Put love and happiness back into your heart.

Like the people you are with. Enjoy your job because some don't have one. Be happy in what you do. It will help your emotional and spiritual health. Anger you have control of the switch. Turn it on or off. It's just an emotion. Be Happy!

Head Shepherd
POG

Spirit
MISTAKES

Corinthians 7:8 For even if I made you sad by my letter, I do not regret having written it (even though I did regret it for I see that my letter made you sad, through only for a short time).

G ood morning people of God We as people of God has all made mistakes, it's just when we make them we must not let them keep us from moving on in life. No one is without sin! When we make mistakes forgive yourself and others who has trespass against you. Learn from your mistakes so you would not make the same one again. God will always forgive you when you make a mistake if you just ask him too. But most people just stay in their same spot not willing to forgive themselves or others for their mistakes. We must move forward with our lives to see what god has In store for us. Mistakes are made when we don't pray about our decision or keep God in what we are doing in life. God knows what is right for you just ask him for some guidance he will show you the right way to go in life. Stop making mistakes and feeling bad about yourself just stay in faith everything will come out alright in life. Then forgive others who have done you wrong. Just have a positive attitude and think of good thoughts that will change your life for the better. Mistakes are there to make you stronger in your faith. Pass the test and move on with your life. Generally, a mistake is a decision or an action – or lack thereof-that we fear we'll come to regret. Mistakes usually cause some degree of pain, loss, or struggle, certainly we might agree that we don't care for the consequences and hence we call it a mistake. The irony is that these events that we try so hard to avoid are sometimes precisely what we need to experience. Ordinarily, growth doesn't occur without some of those challenging feelings we try so hard to avoid.

Head Shepherd
POG

Spirit
MUSIC

Psalm32:7 You are my hiding place, you will protect me from trouble and surround me with songs of deliverance.

Good morning people of God . Music has been around since the beginning of time. There is gospel, blues, jazz, and a lot more variety of music. It can put you into a good mood when you listen to it or motivate you. God says to praise him with a good hymn. The enemy also has his music too that some listen to. We must be careful to what we are listening to when it comes to music. Your children are easily influenced by music. It will get inside their mind and start to control them. There has been studies done when some children said the music makes them do this evil bid. Be careful what you let your children listen to. Whatever you let into your subconscious it will sooner or later manifest itself. Satanic lyrics will begin to control your actions. Have you ever heard someone say the devil made me do it? There are evil forces in the world trying to take you straight to hell. Guard your mind be careful what you listen to. You can actually see the power of music. People who were just sitting there not engaged in anything, light up when they start hearing music from when they were 25. There is nothing wrong with listening to music. Just be careful of the type you are listening to. Music can be a learning tool or it can uplift your spirit. The book of psalms are all different types of lyrics praising our God. Try to read this book then you will know which music is right or wrong.

Head Shepherd P.O.G.
Loving Ministry

Spirit

NEW WAYS!

Two individuals standing on either side of number 9 that has been drawn on the floor. For one person,. It appears as the number 6 and for another is the number 9.Who is right and who is wrong? Obviously They both are right yet they both are wrong in the eyes of another individual, because of the viewing perspective. Both of them considered themselves to be right. Here they must understand the other perspective by changing their sites. If people simply understand that a life perception can be changed molded and explained the world can be better placed for all. It can put an end to fights wars daily quarrels and much more. The only requirement is to see things from another person's perception. It is funny way to help put negative situations, and to proper perspective while all negative events are unpleasant. There is most certainly a difference. If you have an inconsiderate boss while that can make work unpleasant on me. In the occasions it is still a blessing to have employment others feel that their spouse is irresponsible with money but at least you have a spouse who loves. You. . The moment your perspective on life comes to play. All risk remember that it is not the alpha perspective and that the other person perspective matters as well. A person who really wants something will find a way. A person who doesn't will find an excuse! It doesn't matter how hard you get hit it matters. How hard you can get hit and keep moving.

Head Shepherd
P.O.G.
Loving Ministry

Spirit
NEXT LEVEL!

Psalms 26:12 My feet stand on level ground; in the great congregation I will praise the Lord.

People of God is time to elevate our lives. Stop living in these low frequency. Raise your spiritual belief to a higher level. Stop letting men dictate to you telling us how to live our lives. Living from paycheck to paycheck, and chasing after material things. Learn to enjoy the splendor of life like a sunrise, or the moon at night. The true treasures of life is when you love someone, and someone love you back. The enemy old ways of living life we have to change them, and start loving, sharing, and caring for one another. You have to stop living life in these low frequency, and raised the vibration. Elevate yourself out of this three dimension, and go to the next level. Believe in your heart that all of this craziness will pass. Know that you are a child of the most high in all things are possible nothing in this world Can harm you, because you're a supreme being. We are pure energy nothing can delete our light. Stay committed to what is right in life. Don't believe this enemy when he tell you he is trying to do what is right to protect you from harm. He only wants to deceive you so that he can steal your soul. We as people of God need to come together and help each other go to the next level. The true power lies in the body of Christ. We all need to be connected. If we are fearing each other it means that we are not living our true existence of being believers. You must remember his words no weapons formed against you shall never prosper. You must be a warrior of light to defeat this darkness. Evil does not drive back evil only love does. The power of love is the greatest energy in the universe. When we all go to this next level we must remember to love each other just let God guide our life.

Head Shepherd
P.O.G.
Loving Ministry

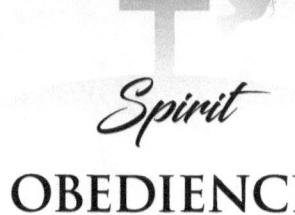

OBEDIENCE

Deuteronomy 8:6 Observe the commands of the Lord your God, walking in obedience to him and revering him.

Compliance with an order, request, or law, or submission, to another authority. Even at birth we are taught obedience by our parents to respect others. To listen to the authority, and do what they tell you. Teacher's, policeman, and government just go along with what they say. When will we be able to make our own decision on how to live our lives? Humans are so confused on how God wants them to live their life. They are being led by what the world want them to do. We look at others who are in power, and try to be like them even though they don't love themselves. Why are you trying to be like someone who don't love you? Be like someone who live their life serving others. Be obedient to God's word live life helping others. When you are able to be obedient to God's word he will give you good things in life. Be consistent, and dedicated, in treating others with respect. Stop letting man lead you in the wrong direction with his fork tongue. When you are being obedient you are no longer living in the ego. You are doing his will. The true measure of a person is how they follow his principles, and his words. We have to overcome the invisible enemy that is in the strong notions in our head. Everything in the world is possible it takes discipline person to make it happen. We generate fears while we sit. We overcome them by action.

Head Shepherd
P.O.G.
Loving Ministry

Spirit OPTIONS

John 14:6 Jesus answered 'I am the way and the truth and the life. No one comes to the father except through me.'

Why do we think there is only one way to accomplish things in life. We just want to give up on the 1st try. This is just the enemy trying to discourage you. Delete these negative thoughts out of your mind. There will always be more than 1 way of doing things in life. With options you have hope. In life we have been taught there's only one answer. There are many ways of doing things in Life. You must be able to think outside of the box believe in your ideas and yourself. When you are able to tap into your full potential. That's when you are able to begin to create things. There is power in your words whenever you speak you can manifest. Stop holding on to that there is only one way of doing things. Claim and seek out the things you want to materialize in your life. Let no stone be overturned You're a unique individual. Stop making excuses, and set out on your venture. Don't let others dictate your destiny. You are in control of your life. There will be many days you will feel you can't go on. When you feel this way never give up because, your about to have your dream. If plans A does not work Then you must move to b or C just keep thriving we are taught as children that there is always more than one way of doing things. There is nothing more beautiful than a person with a made up mind. The moment you stop complaining that's the moment you take control of your life to achieve your dream. With God there will always be many ways of doing things in life. Just stay on the path of righteousness. Success comes when your not afraid. To step out on faith and stand strong in God's words.

Head Shepherd
P.O.G.
Loving Ministry

Spirit

OVERCOME

Romans 12:21 Do not be overcome by evil, but overcome evil with good.

To overcome your problems in life you must first stop being of the world. The world is filled with chaos, and pain. There's so much pressure on us trying to live better than others. Free yourself from other people's opinions, and live your life for Christ. To overcome anything in life you must first think you can. Stop all the worrying and doubting yourself. Be of great cheer we are here with you. When you know others are there for you it become easy to overcome. Take the pressure out of life. Live above your frustrations take some action and believe you can achieve anything that you desire. Problems do not last forever will you take authority over your life? You can't change the past but you can start where you are, and change the ending. People who want a better life is people who response to failure different. They keep on trying when there seemed to be no hope at all. It doesn't matter what others are doing it matters what you are doing in life. Stay away from negative people there is no situation too difficult to overcome in life. You are capable of creating whatever reality you want. Stay focused on Gods words to get you through the difficulties of life. We all need inspiration, and these lines are truly amazing to fuel our motivation. The world will be a much better place if everyone understand their thoughts to create the life they want. Don't worry just remember God is always in control!

Head Shepherd
P.O.G.
Loving Ministry

Spirit
OVERCOMING

To overcome any negative situation. You have to let it go and give yourself a chance to think about it. Anything worth having it must agree with you. In order to be a part of your life. Be selective to who you give your time, and your energy to win life. Life is a struggle. If you aren't like most people you have weaknesses, shortcoming, karma, bad habits and destructive tendencies that you would like to overcome. You have probably tried to rid yourself of these flause and fail perhaps repeatedly. You got to follow your Passion. You've got to figure out what it is you love. Who you really are, and have the courage to do that. I believe that the only courage anybody ever needs is the courage to follow your own heart. Be thankful for what you have you'll end up having more. If you concentrate on what you don't have you will never ever have enough. You will always go through things in this life. It comes a time when you have to stop letting people affect the outcome of your life. Let it go all the bad situations you went though in life. Forgive and move on with your life. Sometimes God doesn't give you what you want not because you didn't deserve it, but just because you deserve much better. Things will change when you start looking at yourself differently, and start seeing the good in yourself. When we strive to become better than everything around us becomes better too.

Head Shpherd
P.O.G.
Loving Ministry

Spirit

ONE OF THESE DAYS!

Proverbs 12:27 the lazy person does not roast prey, but personal possession are precious to the diligent.

Good morning people of God. Peoples of God are always saying one of these days I am going to do this. To make my life better. Why put off what you can do today and not tomorrow. If you want something in life you must ask first then believe that the father will give it to you. Write it down have a goal, and an action plan on how you will achieve it. You must think like it has already happened for you. See it in your mind 24/24 live it till the full. The power of the universe will attract what you think about the most. It is like a magnet. Positive thoughts will always come true with deep belief in them. Faith is like hopping for the unknown just knowing the heavenly father will make it happen for you. One of these days can be today. Just walk out in faith and start believing in yourself. Knowing that God is there right by your side showing you the way to go. People will try to tell you this is not right, but they are trying to keep you where they are. You must rise and go higher in life. Be around people you would like to be like. P.O.G. is a great start. The road to having a great life will always be filled with blockers. You must be strong in your mind able to move around them. God promise he will guide you through all life obstacles just believe this. One of these days will come soon with this thought. One of the biggest reasons why people procrastinate is because they see catastrophize, or make a Hugh deal out of something. It may be related to how tough, how boring, or how painful it will be to complete the task the underlining theme is that doing a task will be unbearable." We must remember with no pain there is no gain. "The secret of getting things done is act."

Head Shepherd
P.O.G.

Spirit
PASSING BY

Time is passing so quickly I encourage you to live your life to the fullest. The future has not been promised to anyone so enjoy the day. Live your life like you are in a movie. You are the director, writer, and like the star. Live like you choose to live and not let others opinion affect your decision. Stop fearing the unknown, and explore the world. See all of the beauty that God has created the mountain, the seas, and the forest are all like a wonderful dream. Sometimes it seems as if life is passing us by. When we are children time filled with endless car journeys, and summer holidays which seem to last forever. But as an adult time seems to speed up at a frightening rate, with Christmas and birthdays arriving more quickly every year. Success at anything will always come down to this focus and effort. and we control both. You are your only competition trust yourself and trust a process. Take time to live life one out every day at least to hear the bird singing, read a good book, see a fine movie, and if it were possible to speak a few reasonable words. Never stop believing in yourself. Keep moving forward. Nothing is more than you can handle. It is just more than you expected. Push through. Do the work and get it done. Don't be afraid to start all over. Again This time you are not starting from scratch. You are starting from experience. Try not to become a person of success, but rather try to become a person of value.

Head Shepherd
P.O.G.
Loving Ministry

Spirit
PATIENCE

To accept or tolerate delay, trouble or suffering without getting angered or upset. Experts want you to know that even though we all very when it comes to how much patience we might naturally bring to any given situation, we can all work on it and improve. Some people are naturally athletic and others are less inclined, but even the most nonathletic person can train and get better, no matter what base level you start from. The same is the cause with patience with practice you can get better responding with patience. Personality plays a role in why some of us tend to respond to life delays, and setbacks with more calm than other. Studies have shown for example that people who are more conscientious agreeable and open to new experience tend to have more patience, and people who have fewer of those traits tend to be more likely to be impatient . Just keep going don't stop, don't give up until you win trust me whatever you push so hard you will get it. It's 100% sure that You are a born winner and it's our father's wish in heaven that you are successful in your life. And be patient it is important for good results. Patience is the key to victory. Work hard, pray, and be prepared never give up. You can't lose if you refuse to quit! Keep going! Keep moving forward!

Head Shepherd
P.O.G.
Loving Ministry

Spirit
PEACE

John 16:33 I have told you these things, so that in me you may have peace. In this world you will have trouble. But take heart! I have overcome the world.

Good morning my P.O.G. family. From the beginning of time there has been no peace on earth. This Devil just want to keep us in fear, and hating each other. There are those who feed off this negative energy. Even today he has not given up on trying to control the world. He has us in a psychological war fare trying to steal our soul. Just filling the universe with all this negative energy. We need to learn how to transform this energy back to positive. By stopping living from generation to generation of fearing, and hating each other. When we are able to stop being of the world, and start living a righteous life. Then the father will change your perception of life. Then you will be able to remain calm in a storm. We must stop seeing ourselves as a color, and start seeing ourselves as a human being. It is the sun that change our skin. We are all created the same A peaceful mind will give you a peaceful life. God says you should live a calm, and modest life. Let love guide you through the tribulations of life. Stay peaceful,and hopeful things will be alright. YOUR EVERLASTING LIFE.

Head Shepherd
P.O.G.
Loving Ministry

Spirit

PERSISTENCE

We all go through hard times once in a while but don't give up keep on going! The outcome will be rewarding. We were all born to be game changers, but the difference is who decides to give up along the way, and who decides to work hard despite any failure, or inconveniences. It is important to stay positive, and keep pushing yourself. You never know what you're going to do end up with, but if you push through the tough times you might find success. Persistence is probably one of the most admirable characteristics a person can possess is the ability to be determined to do, or achieve something regardless of any set back. A distinguishing attribute of those who succeed in life against those who don't persist. Many has the capacity to set goals, and plans towards success. Yet only few succeed, because only few stick to work on their goals, and plans until it is accomplished. Developing resistance is a master skill to success it is easier to relax, and do nothing or just live in our comfort zone rather than face the uncertainty, and discomfort or sailing through our goals. Beside the idea of failure, and hardship is unbearable but if you want to create change in your life, and achieve success now is the time to develop a master persistence. Proverbs pr chapter 4 versus 25 through 26 let your eyes look directly forward and your gaze be straight before you ponder the path of your feet then all your ways will be sure, however small or insignificant that step might seem. Do it. Do that little piece

Head Shepherd
P.O.G.
Loving Ministry

Spirit

PERSPECTIVE

Whenever your views of life are off, you needed it to seek spiritual counseling. Various counseling skill can be learned and developed to foster and maintain the psychological process, including good communication problem solving, and goal setting, and introduce coping technique such as self talk and visualization. Most therapists and counselors would agree that a good counseling relationship is fundamental to being effective with clients. Such alliances build on several counselor offered qualities, core conditioning, and skills, including empathetic understanding, respect, and acceptance for clients, current states of being and congruence or genuineness you can turn your life around you can go through hell, and back. It is possible never underestimate yourself. Always believe in you always remember that persistence and not giving up is the key to achieving goals and positive change in life. Life will never go exactly as we want it to. And people will never behave the way we expect them to behave. The Thing in life isn't perfect, and it never will be. People will hurt you, lie to you, cheat on you, and they will do you wrong, because everyone is at a different spiritual awareness point in their life journey. People will come into your life for A reason and a season and a lifetime. And will each carry with them a lesson that will elevate you to the best you providing that you get the lesson. In spite of all that life is a beautiful journey. We only have to see the beauty in the bumps along the way. In order to survive the most challenging points in our lives, sometimes all we have to do is to take ownership of our thoughts and know that we have the ability to change our perspective at any time.

Head Shepherd
P.O.G.
Loving Ministry

Spirit

PLANNING

Jeremiah 26:3 Perhaps they will listen and each will turn from their evil ways. Then I will relent and not inflict on them the disaster. I was planning because, of the civil they have done.

Good morning people of God. Most people today are not willing to make any type of plans for their life. They just go thorough life letting things happen without any say in it. We wonder why we can't get ahead in life. If you were to ask any successful person how they did it they will tell you with a plan of action. There are some who know that something is about to happen in life but yet they do not prepare for it. Planning is the key to everything in life if you want to be successful at it. Isn't it funny how you would plan for dinner, but not for your future. When you plan for things it takes away some of the unknowns in life. Don't be a last minute planner, because it will be so much that can go wrong. You should plan with a clear, calm mindset of seeing it happening for you. Planning is like asking God for something in advance knowing that he will make this happen for you. You want to do some planning early. The rule of thumb is to do as much early planning as it takes to convince yourself the project will work. You don't need to know every detail. You just need to convince yourself somehow or other, it will work. When some plans don't work just learning to adapt, and going with the flow is probably the most widely used skill in the world. People who don't plan are planned to fail in life. Your life will not get better by hoping but by planning instead. Your plan should be like a road map for your life. Write it down in detail making a clear, and specific. From time to time look it over, and make sure you are going in the right direction. And when your not just turn on your GOD.

Head Shepherd
P.O.G.
Loving Ministry

Spirit
POWERFUL

You are a spirit filled with magnetic energy. You are able to manifest whatever reality you choose it to be!. Step into your power, and be that creator who you were created to be. Being powerful requires a deep understanding of yourself analyzing your strength, weakness, opportunities, and threats let you trigger your decision. Making skills. self-awareness can help you manage your emotions, make better decisions, and build stronger relationships with others. Your personality can influence how you relate to others, and how they perceive you. People with powerful personalities inspire others to emulate them, and have the respect of those around them. Many people with powerful personalities are successful entrepreneurs. They're innovative persuasive ambition, self-discipline, and confident. Their resilience enables them to face challenges, and recover from setbacks. A person with a strong personality is typical c influential, or inspirational. The idea of having to feel influential and respected is a natural trait of every human being. Authentically were created to have dominion and control over the earth.

For our struggle is not against flesh and blood, but against the powers of the dark world, and against the spiritual forces of evil in the heavenly realms. May the God of hope fill you with all joy, and peace as you trust in him, so that you may overflow with hope by the power of the holy spirit.

Head Shepherd
P.O.G.
Loving Ministry

Spirit
POSSESSIONS

2 Chronicles 1:11 God said to Solomon, since this is your year hearts desire and you have not asked for wealth, possessions or honor, nor asked for a long life but for wisdom and knowledge to govern my people over whom I have made you King.

Good morning people of God. Why is it that people put so much value in things and not people? We spend our whole life accumulating things of value. Never worried about our family, and friends who are around us. We put so much thought in the things we want to buy, and never about how your people are doing. We never think about how we should treat people when we need them. We just say, and do whatever comes to our mind. Our possession we make sure that we take really good care of them, and never once thinking how we can take care of the elderly in homes. Our possessions has demonized us, and made us into a selfish cult of people always thinking about one's self first. If you can remember not long ago back in the 1800's a man could be another mans possession even in the bible days .Jesus told this man that wanted to follow him that if he gives up all his worldly possession that he could. But the man had so many worldly possessions he just turned and walked away. There is so much going on in the world today we must stop,and see what is the purpose of thee. God put us here to beautify this world. By loving, caring, and sharing with each other. He says to love thy enemy as they love themselves. So P.O.G. stop putting so much value on your things. Be a people of giving and doing for one another. Then your heavenly father will help us with what is about to come. If you do not know about the future of being selfish people I advise you to read the book of revelations. The end time is near so help your children, and your friends be ready for the rapture. I was once told if you do not remember the pass you are doom to repeat it.

Head Shepherd
P.O.G.
Loving Ministry

Spirit

POWER OF NICENESS

....

"What lies in our power," to do, lies in our power not to do.' Life-and-death is in the power of the tongue.'"Speak life over yourself and others. There is no complicated secret to working well with others. You get you just have to learn to appreciate them! First you practice recognizing someone's value, and contributions. Then you make a habit of telling them. {Thank you} People feel appreciated when you point out the detail of their work. Simply telling them they did a good job isn't enough. It's better to say I'm proud of you for doing this specific thing. It's hard not to notice great attitudes in the world filled with bad attitudes. When you call attention to the passion and enthusiasm of others. It renews their energy, and sparks new energy in others. You'll end up having more people helping you with the vision God gives you. Many people in my life have gone above and beyond to serve others, and do their jobs well. And It's given me great joy to point out their contributions, and tell them how much they are appreciated. Sometimes it's a conversation. But it's become a habit to notice the efforts and attitude of others, recognized their perseverance, and encouraged them to keep going. It takes practice to live with in attitude of gratitude and a spirit of appreciation. You can start practicing. Your mind is a fight for territory if you don't fight for what you want what you don't want will automatically take over. Know that you are enough. And the only thing that's stopping you is you. Be nice to people, then they will be nice to you.

Head Shepherd
P.O.G.
Loving Ministry

Spirit

POWERLESS

Romans 5:6 You see just the right time when we were still powerless Christ died for the ungodly.

Good morning people of God. Have you ever felt powerless like the lost of a job, or a love one, or the doctor had diagnosed you with a certain amount of time to live? It gives you a sense of hopelessness things that are out of your control. You have been living your whole life being a man, or women in charge of your life. Now things are out of your hand, and a feeling of failure sets in. You start to question everything about your existence, and you start to have all these different emotions. You begin to question your faith is there really a God? Why would he put me through this? I am a good person. I pray, I go to church, I pay my tithes. Why must I go through this? You must remember faith is the unseen, and the unknown. Remember in the bible there was a man name Job he was loyal to Gods word, and he was a rich man. He lost everything his family, his home, his business he was conflicted with an illness, but yet he kept his faith in God. I know you say yeah, but still why me? I am just a common man. You must remember when you believe you must do it in all situations good or bad. The mystery of the universe is something man will never solve. What God decides to do in your life you must believe it is something to better you. In life there will always be death, and lost of someone or something. This is how the universe function in spring everything is in bloom, and in the fall it dies and go away. We all are creation of the almighty father. When things become difficult you just don't understand just kneel, and pray and ask your father for wisdom to get you through. Your father loves you with unconditional love. He will never give you more than what you can bare. He just wants you to be a warrior for Christ, and show others the way to the light.

Head Shepherd
P.O.G.
LovingMinistry

Spirit
PRACTICE WHAT YOU PREACH

....

2 Timothy 4:2 Preach the word, be prepared in season and out of season; correct, rebuke and encourage – with great patience and careful instruction.

There are so many in society today. That can tell you so quickly how to live your life. They always think they have the right solution to your problem. Have you ever stop, and notice that they're telling you what to do, but they are not. That is the problem in the world today. The authorities think they have the answers to everything. But yet they don't seem to follow what they say. It seemed to be two sets of rules do as I say not as I do. They tell you it is for your safety. We just want to protect you from harm. They tell you to cover your face, so you can protect your grandparents. But all the while you're weakening your immune system. They want to inject you with these toxins. Which will make you more sicker. If the authority is really concerned about your health. Why don't they practice what they preach. Be the first one to take the injections. This enemy is just testing you to see how much you would do his foolishness. When someone is truly concerned about you. They would tell you how to protect yourself. Like boost your immune system with a vitamin C or vitamin D. Get out in the sun and take a walk. God has given you ears, eyes, and you must decipher who's telling you the truth. When a person is genuine about your health. They will put their health in the line of harm before they put yours. Someone of God will always put his people first, because that is what Christ would do. Don't listen to someone words but to their action. Then you will know the real leader.

Head Shepherd
P.O.G.
Loving Ministry

Spirit
PROSPERITY

The state of being prosperous. You can achieve prosperity through dedication, and hard work. How do we define our success.? Is it because we get a big paycheck, live in an extraordinary large home, married the hottest guy or girl in the country, or drive the fastest car on the block? Building a business, and entrepreneurship requires unique talents, and a love for your career. Its not about frivolous things. Its about opportunity, and your ability to uncover your dreams, and do what you love. If you don't love it then why do it? Don't let the fear of losing be greater then the excitement of winning. Nothing happens until something moves. Yes nothing happens until you take action your life is your personal responsibility, and you have to treat it so! Being realistic is the most common path to mediocrity. In order to succeed we must first believe that we can. Some people have a positive attitude, and some have a negative attitude, and that makes every person unique from one another. A person with a positive attitude always get so much attention for their good behavior, but a person with a negative attitude don't. People are so obsessed with what they don't have that they never allow themselves to be satisfied with what they do have in life. Constantly having a mindset of wanting more, and more will squash any chances you have of acceptance. Embrace acceptance and watch your life be alright.

Head Shepherd
P.O.G.
Loving Ministry

Spirit PEACE OF MIND

....

Philippians 4:17 and the peace of God that surpasses all understanding will guard your hearts and minds in Christ Jesus.

Good morning people of God. People of God we must have a peace of mind all the time. Stop letting the devil get inside your head and taking your peace of mind. Life is filled with situations out of our control. Being mad and upset about them will not make things better for you. We need God so we can keep our peace of mind. When you are calm things will make more since to you. A clear head will bring good thoughts and you will make the right decision. Life is so confusing people are trying to tell you what is right from wrong. But only God knows what is right for you in life. Ask him to clear your minds so that you will know what is right to do in life. Peace is hard to find here on earth there is so much conflict going on everywhere. People are not showing love towards one another instead just hating each other. Our communities are filled with violence, crime, and murder. Families are being torn apart by divorce and infidelity. It's difficult to find a peace of mind with all things going on. God has promised if you ask for peace and believe it with all your heart you will have it. Stop worrying about all the bad things going on in life. Stay focus on the father and be at peace with yourself. There's already enough bad in the world we need more good, so show some compassion towards each other. Where there is love there is peace in the world. Peace of mind is something we all seem to want, and want more of. Few of us got it, and when we do it tends to be fleeting. I think the reason has something to do with how we think of "Peace of mind". It is not something we can have and hold, but it is certainly something that we can learn to cultivate and allow to grow. Allow yourself time to just sit, without distractions, without something to do, or a place to go. No multitasking. Use this time for you and get curious about your mind and experience just as it is. Look into your experience and just watch the goings on between your ears and in your heart. There is nothing to do no state to achieve. Just practice being exactly where you are just as you are. Meditate on God's word and repeat in a whisper God give me peace over and over again.

Head Shepherd
P.O.G.

Spirit
PRIDE

....

Proverbs 29:23 a person's pride will bring him low, but one who has a lowly spirit will gain honor.

Good morning people of God. Today most all people are too proud to ask for help from others. Our pride has made us not needing anyone. Some are embarrassed to ask someone to help them, even if they're hungry, hurting and have no place to stay. But yet their pride keeps them from asking for a helping hand. There is no one that doesn't need help at one point in their life. We are not machines but humans made to make mistakes. When the bad things in life happened to you don't be ashamed to ask for some help from others. There have been many whose pride has kept them from something great in life. There pride is saying you don't need God. You need God with whatever you do in life. This nation was not just built by one man but many. Start wanting others to be a part of sharing their lives with you. When there is more than one you have more ideas to consider. God says there is strength in unity. Who are we with our arrogance and pride thinking we don't need God. He is the reason you are here on earth. He is the alpha and the omega. We should be ashamed of ourselves for thinking this way. Your pride will stop you all the time from his glory. You were created to help one another and show love to everybody this is your purpose in life. Pride has a pretty negative reputation. After all it's one of the seven deadly sins. All of us should be aware of hubristic pride creeping in; otherwise, success may come at the cost of being nice. President Obama has tended to avoid arrogance speech and to acknowledge the roll of others in his accomplishments this brand of self – regards illustrates the positives of pride for the rest of us. It motivates us to achieve and can feel our lives with meaning. Experimental evident supports the notion that pride that results from a job well done encourage future success. the more you feel authentic pride " the more you're going to try to achieve. P.O.G. let's stop the self love and start showing the world we are a creation of God who loves humanity.

Head Shepherd
P.O.G.
Loving Ministry

Spirit
PURPOSE

....

What's your purpose in life? Do you know where you're going, do you like what you're doing? Your purpose is why you are here on this Earth. God-created each one of us to be a creator. If you refuse to give up there is no such thing as failure, and you will eventually claim your victory, stay strong! Once you develop yourself everything else will fall into place. Discipline yourself, and you will be able to get what you want in life. Make your time work worthwhile. Make your life Worthwhile. And always put God 1st in your life! Your own beliefs are the most powerful forces that influence your existence. They determine what you perceive and how you perceive it.. They influence your thoughts your expectations and your actions. They shape your personality they even affect the outcome of your action, and the way others perceive and respond to you. No matter how much it hurts you now someday you will look back and realize your struggles change your life for the better. We have to stop being victim, stop creating self impose limitations, and stop the excuses. Let's make a commitment to change for the better otherwise nothing will change. You become what you digest into your spirit. Whatever you think about focus on, read about, talk about you're going to attract more of it into your life. Make sure they're all positive.

Head Shepherd
P.O.G.
Loving Ministry

Spirit QUEST

Jeremiah 29:13 when you seek me in prayer and worship, you will find me available to you. If you seek me with all your heart and soul.

Good morning people of God. We as P.O.G. must be on a quest in life. Looking for the good things like love, happiness, and peace. We must first learn to love yourself before you can love anyone else. Stop all the shade throwing, and hating others just because you don't know anything about them. We should be a society of compassionate people, and caring about one another. Love each other as god loves you. Be happy put a smile on your face each and every day. Stop worrying about life. God has promised he will take care all your needs if you just believe in him. Forgive those who have done wrong to you. Take the power back from them being able to make you angry when you see them. Have an attitude of happiness all the time it is good for your soul. Being happy is the best medicine you can take. You will have longevity if you are happy all the time. Life will always attract happy people around you all the time. "Wouldn't that be nice?" There has been no peace on earth every since Eve bit into the apple. Peace of mind nowadays is something that is hard to have. There is so much violence, and hatred, in the world today. People are scared to come out of their homes. Worrying all the time that something bad may happen to them. This country is so corrupt people don't know who they can trust anymore. Hunger, homeless, and sickness, is everywhere. How can there be peace with all of these things going on in life? The key to peace and well - being is to accept life as it is. -Unpleasantlessness included- and then to be as present for it as we can. When we're present in this way, compassion naturally arises from any suffering we might be experiencing. A mind that is equanimous understands that life is a mixture of joy, and sorrow, and responds to both those circumstance with an even temper, and a peaceful heart. When we are able to follow Gods laws and principles. Then only you will have these things that we seek.

Head Shepherd
P.O.G.
Loving Ministry

Spirit
RACISM

Proverbs 10:12 Hatred stirs up conflict, but love covers over all wrongs.

Good morning my P.O.G. family. Racism in America has existed since the colonial era This was such an uncomfortable topic to write about. You would think that by now we would have overcome being submerged in the mist, gestures of hatred. I would never think that we would have a president who concur with different groups of people with such hate in their hearts. You know whats disturbing that everyone of us at some point will be subjected to this type of behavior. We are taught racism by our parents, and that hate is passed down from generation to generation. Most youth don't understand why they hate someone, because who the person is. The enemy does not want peace on earth,because when there is love in the world he has no power over us. I remember as a youth my father moved us from the west side to the north side. I was in 8th grade in a school that was called hate. There was this white gang who called themselves the KKK. They were all teenagers. They would come to our house at night, and break out the windows, and call us the n word. It went as far as them burning a cross on our front lawn. Where do you think these kids learned this hate from? We need to stop hating each other, because of the color of our skin. There is more to a person if you just take the time to get to know them. God did not create no one to be better than someone else we are all created in his image. Even in today's society racism it still rear its ugly head. I will never forget 911. The hospital sent all employees home early that day. We were taking the bus home, and before I crossed the street there was this Muslim kid being attacked by a bunch of thugs. They were throwing pop cans at him. When I yelled for them to stop they fled off in their car. The kid would not let me call the police he was afraid that he will get mistreated. I will never forget that day. It was such a shock to me, because I work in such a diverse area well ad least I thought. I believe if we were to live our lives as

Jesus taught to love your enemies as you love yourself. We must stop, and recondition ourselves by not believing in the things that we were taught we know that are wrong. I know that it is hard to teach an old dog new tricks, but think about this would you want anyone to hate your child, because of who they are? I think not. Its time to make a difference,and make this world a better place. Start seeing the beauty in the world just be more polite to others, and stop putting your needs first, and think of others. When you live a life of serving others you live your life as Christ lived his life, when he was here on earth. Parents start educating your children to have tolerance for one another. To stop the hate just do the opposite that is to love.

Head Shepherd & Lady Shepherd
P.O.G.
Loving Ministry

Spirit REFLECTION

1 Corinthians 13:12 For now we see only a reflection as in a mirror; then we shall see face to face. Now I know in part; then I shall know fully, even as I am fully known.

Good morning my P.O.G. family. Every since we are being forced to stay in our homes we have had nothing, but time to reflect back on our lives. We have taken so much for granted by not being grateful for what we have. Like just spending times with others to just talk about life. The little things in life seems so precious right now. A walk on the beach going to the store with out fear, or just going to a sporting event. This enemy has taken so much. We can't even go to church to spend time in prayer together. When you are able to look back over your life. The difficult time does not seem very hard right now. All the trials, and tribulations in life cannot compare to this moment in life. We have been told to give up our freedoms to let satan rule over us.. We are warriors for Christ no weapons formed against us shall prosper. It's time to stop being afraid, and let the light inside of you shine. Stand up, and fight for your rights. Take back what they are trying to take away from you. That is your dignity and pride. We were given right to let no domestic or foreign enemy to take away our freedoms. God created each and every one of us to have compassion for humanity. Don't let this devil take control of this world. Activate the power within your heart to drive him back with love. There is a thing called tough love that is what we must do to defeat this enemy. We must go through this storm. Remember no pain no gain. It's time we learn self knowledge of ourselves. He has the keys in the end we win.

Head Shepherd
P.O.G
LovingMinistry

Spirit
RELENTLESS

If you honor where you are with your best effort even if it's not it will lead you to it. Keep your face always toward the sun shine, and shadows will fall behind you. Showing or promising no abandonment of severity, intensity, karma strength, or pace. To achieve any major dream or goal you have to be relentless. In other words, when you're relentless you don't back down, give in or give up or accept less, and a lot of people don't like the idea of being relentless, because it isn't nice compromising, considerate, or friendly.. Here's some news you weren't put on this earth to be nice. You were put on this Earth to fulfill your mission, and the fulfillment of any mission is going to require being relentless at some point in time.

Good or bad being relentless is a core part of my being.. And its a double edge sword or maybe its just one coin with 2 sides.. Relentless means never giving up until you get what you want, but it also means you may disregard the consequence, and hurt some people along the way. Results 1st always. Let your mind be at peace, and create your own reality in life. Never let anyone take you off your path in life. Thinking positively and invest on it you will see the beauty on how you will grow quickly. Don't be limited by what others say about you. Be willing to take risk, and be open to making mistakes. The sorrow, anger, and pain will soon fade and will fade away. When you have God and a positive mind in life.

Head Shepherd
P.O.G.
Loving Ministry

Spirit

RIGHT ENERGY

People take different road seeking fulfillment and happiness. Just because they're not on your road doesn't mean they're gotten lost. The strength and vitality required for sustained physical or mental activity. Energy is the life blood of our everyday decision and action. It is also the fundamental key that goes into creating a well balanced, rounded, and fulfilling lifestyle. The simple truth is that without adequate amount of energy, nothing can really be achieved, no true pleasures can be experienced or enjoyed. And no effective, and well-thought-out decisions can be made. Stay on top of your emotions by being present in the moment. Read your thoughts and the feelings you are projecting out into the world at all times, and most importantly avoid the habit of permitting which triggers many self inflicted negative states of being. You cannot control what happened to you but you can control your attitude towards what happens to you, and in that you will be mastering change rather than allowing it to master you. Whatever lifestyle you choose to live it's in the energy you put toward creating that reality. We are all frequencies of energy be on a timeline of happiness. Don't let negative people, and negative things drain you of your energy. Be around people with the same energy level as you are at. The more positive people you are around straight the stronger you become. Feed your mind body with positive things and grow into someone incredible.

Head Shepherd
P.O.G.
Loving Ministry

Spirit

ROYALTY

P.O.G you're people of excellence. You are the rulers over the land. We must know our true selves. Take back the power which was stolen. Improve yourself to become better, but don't let it be ego driven. Become the best version of you on, all levels have ambitions, and goals. When we have to do something. We shouldn't postpone it. Leave it for tomorrow, but we should do it today, now because we don't. Even know if we will be around tomorrow! Put your imagination to work, and write a short story about what you would do. If you were royalty. What would you title be? What type of country would you rule over? What would you enjoy most about being royalty? What things would annoy you about being royalty? Have fun and, Be sure to share your story with the friends, or family. Change will come by working together and making it easier to embrace decisions that will sustain our world rather than carry on as though there are no limits, Or as though our actions have no consequences. Forgive me for my boldness in coming out here, the Lord will surely reward you with eternal royalty for your descendants for you are fighting his battles, and you will never do wrong throughout your entire life. For his Holy Spirit speaks to us deep in our hearts and tells us that we are God's children. and since we are his children we will share his treasures. By turning to the one who has the power to help you change God because of him, you can become more than you ever thought possible. through his grace and healing power. You can rise above sin and regrets overcome obstacles and improve your life every day.

Head Shepherd
P.O.G.
Loving Ministry

Spirit

RIGHT PERSPECTIVE

Our ability to handle life's challenges is a measure of our strengths of characters. The immensity of life finds full expression in our physical bodies. Scientists are unraveling the biological complexity behind our physical existence. Besides this there is a tangible part of our being we are yet to uncover. It lies within reach of everyone. The mind is only a small part of the inner world. The value of that untapped potential that lies in the internal landscape is immeasurable. The mind can be a facilitator or a hurdle. It becomes a facilitator when there is inward freedom from the ego. The perspective we carry can make or break access to inner freedom. Developing the right attitude is both an art an a continual <u>effort.</u> <u>It</u> makes life more enjoyable, satisfying, and is a shortcut to happiness. No perspective is wrong. To tell someone their perspective is wrong is to tell them their experience is wrong. A perspective does not have right or wrong attributes. Perspective can be well informed or a little informed. They can clear or blurry. They can be painful or joyous. But in the end a perspective is the lens that people look through, and lenses can't be wrong. How ever the conclusions that are drawn from perspective can certainly be inaccurate conclusion based on perspective are the things that need shaping, molding, disciplining, and cleaned up not people's perspective. We are to be in a community of people whose perspective are all vastly different, and where we all shape each other's conclusions. Everyone is entitled to their own perspective on anything, but perspective doesn't equal truth. Everyone perspective is true just maybe not the conclusions they are drawing from them.

Head Shepherd
P.O.G.
Loving Ministry

Spirit SATISFIED

What is it going to cost you if you don't. A person who has committed a mistake, and doesn't correct it is committing another mistake. No matter how many things you accumulate in life, of these worldly goods you will never be totally satisfied until you are satisfied with who you are inside. You must be happy with who you was created to be! It is our general feeling about our life, and how pleased we are with how it's going. There are many factors that contribute to life's satisfaction from a number of domains. Including work, romantic relationships, relationships with family, and friends, personal development, health, and wellness and others. Being satisfied and feeling fulfilled are what we all ultimately strive for. Happiness with our lives is the very reason we do not just about anything. So ask yourself. Am I really satisfied with my life? If the answer is no It's time to reevaluate, and change. To lead a satisfying life. Take some time to reflect on the things you have done with your life. Are you living your purpose in life? Are you living your dreams in life? You either going through a storm, or coming out of a storm. You must still stay focused to achieve the things that you want in life. At some point in life you must know what you want in life. Stop letting others opinions define who you are stay committed to yourself. It comes down to one thing are you willing to do the necessary work on a consistent long term basis? Stand up for yourself, and stop hoping others will do it for you!

Head Shepherd
P.O.G.
Loving Ministry

Spirit
SET BACK

Romans 5:5 And hope does not put us to shame, because God's love has been poured out into our hearts through the holy spirit, who has been given to us.

Good morning people of God. Whenever things are going along well in life. There seems to be a set back at some point. That's because the devil does not want you to have what God has promised you already. You must not stop yourself from believing that God wants you to have this. Keep the faith knowing that this will work out for you. Set backs are a big part of life they are there to make your faith stronger. Don't shut down, and give up keep pressing forward going towards your dream. Your mind cannot be unfocused for one moment. In fact disappointment, heartbreak, loss, mistake, unanswered prayers will happen to all of us. It is the human experience. Those who experience very little in their lives appears to have it all they live charmed lives ad least that is how it looks. The reality is we all have pain, and it is all related to our own life experience at any point and time. God knows what we are going through. Just believe in him he will bring you through the storm. Stand strong and know you will make it through. Your heavenly father wants you to have all your hearts desire in life. When ever there is a set back in life know that this will pass. Love yourself and help others in life. Whatever you put out in the universe it will always come back to you. So do good whenever you can. And good things will happen for you.

Head Shepherd
P.O.G.
LovingMinistry

Spirit
SEE LIFE

B eing positive does not mean ignoring the negative being positive means overcoming the negative. Have you ever awaken to the melodies of the bird singing at sunrise? From there branches deep in the trees, they bring a sense of newness, calmness, and inner peace. If only there was a blueprint for life to give us daily guidance, and directions to where to go. What to do, and how To do things the right way. We just have to open our eyes. Open our hearts. And opened our minds to see things beautiful in life. To not just go through things but to grow through every single event in our Life. There is opportunities for everybody. How you perceive every single situation or problem will determine your reality. Focus on you and start doing what you must, what is necessary. Living life for me represents embracing life one moment at a time. We are driven culture, and because of that we focused too much on the future. By doing that we miss what is happening in the present. Realize that people don't think about you as much as you think they do. Don't waste time thinking about what people may, or may not be thinking. Be who you are, no matter who you are with. Always be true to yourself even when it makes you uncomfortable. The meaning of life is to learn how to see the face of God and everyone we have ever met or we'll ever meet. The meaning of life. Is to learn to love it the way it is, to practice peace!

Head Shepherd
P.O.G.
Loving Ministry

Spirit
SEEK GOD FIRST

1 Chronicles 16:10 Glory in his holy name: let hearts of these who seek the Lord rejoice.

Good morning people of God. Why do people seek wealth, power, and fame before God? We spend our entire life from high school to the grave chasing these things. We have been tricked by the social media to want to have these worldly things in life. This is the enemy number one tool social media to deceive us. Its always programmed into our own mind to believe a big home, a luxury automobile, and fine jewelry, will make us happy in life. God has so much in store for you if you just seek him. Your heavenly father will pour out blessings upon you. When you have faith in knowing his son died for you. There will be nothing he won't do for you. Read your bible, and pray asking him you will like to get to know him better. The kingdom of God is where you want to end up,at the end of life. Follow his words, and commandments. Then all things will be possible again. When you seek him your enemy will become your footstool. Change the way you think about life. Put your mind on his words and everything will be alright. Some might object that not to have a predetermine purpose is, really not to have any purpose at all. However, this is to believe that for something to have a purpose, it must have been created with that purpose in mind, and that something that was created with a purpose in mind must necessarily have that very purpose for which it was created. Seek your heavenly father, and believe in yourself with compassion in your heart. Then the things you think that you want to have in life will not be so hard to obtain.

Head Shepherd
P.O.G.
Loving Ministry

Spirit

SELF MASTERY

Self-discipline is the number one trait needed to accomplish your goals. It's the key to sustainable long-term success in all aspects of life. It's about having the ability to control your impulses to stay focused on what matters the most. You have to be able to control your mind in order to master anything in your life. Self-mastery is a lifestyle, and it keeps you out of trouble, it keeps your priority straight. When you absolutely know what you want to achieve, and you are comfortable with the price You have to pay, you realize self mastery is not an option. You can't win the war against the world. If you can't win the war against your own mind. You could fail at what you don't want, so you might as well take a chance on doing what you love. Stop letting others tell you who you are, and focus on what you want in life. It is our light, not our darkness that most frightens us. The most important thing is to be happy in life. And with your life. Happiness comes with success, and you can only gain success If you have self-mastery. We all want to be a master in what we do master means perfection the best. The pro! People pay to watch you do what you do! Master of life requires both repetition and change. You doing something as good as your personality can do it and, then change has to happen. Delay in change cause confusion. Our entire culture up to the invention of the internet was based on repetition. Evolution is going on, and evolution is based on small improvements over repetition. Repetition is good because it leads to mastery someone opinion of you. Doesn't have to be your reality.

Head Shepherd
P.O.G.
Loving Ministry

Spirit
SERVICE

We were created to serve service is a vital part of our essence. Whatever we choose to do in our lifetime all vocations are committed to service. The implies exposing ourselves to the differences and challenges of our own personalities a challenge from which if we seek harmony we all benefit. We attract people who think alike and share our same beliefs. Our actions have the ability to impact our environment around us. Doing well is undoubtedly the meaning of good results, but there is a fundamental factor that energizes the most complex circumstances our own thoughts. We are all deeply interconnected, and rely upon one another for support, acceptance, validation, and above all else love. For that reason the intention you have within your heart have a ripple effect on others they can either help or hurt. To truly be in service to others mean to look inward, and recognize what kind of energy you're putting forth and re-calibrate yourself so that the impact you have on others Creates the kind of change you want to see in the world.

Head Shepherd
P.O.G
Loving Ministry

Spirit
SERVANT

Genesis 18:3 He said my lord," if I have found favor in your sight, do not pass by and leave your servant.

Good morning people of God. People of God must learn to be servants to others. God says "Truly I tell you, just as you did it to one of the least of thee who are members of my family, you did it to me. We are called to love others and love God above all else. It's not about money when you think about helping others. Just some of your time well spent doing something for them. Like taking someone to their appointment, cooking a meal for them or just hanging out and listening to them. We must be willing to help out where needed in life. This world is filled with chaos and pain. People are looking for help. Let's stop being selfish and start putting other people needs before ours. When you are able to do this God will always take care of your needs. We often assume our lives and our futures are in our own hands. Ultimately however, they are in God's hands. Our lives, our bodies, our abilities, and our possessions are all gifts from God. We must be able to share these things with others so Gods plans will become reality. We are a society of me me me people. We need to show more concern about others in life. Everyone has different situations in life when things turn out wrong. There is hardly anyone they can turn to for help. P.O.G. should be about helping all Gods people when and where they need help. If everyone had this mentality then the world will be a much better place. Just a simple smile to one another can make someone feel better about their day. Money has made us all only want it and doing for yourself. God didn't create money he created man. He wants us to love and help one another in life. Be a servant of people, and not money.

Head Shepherd
P.O.G.
Loving Ministry

Spirit SHINING

Take care of the most important thing in your life. You'll have nothing to worry about after! if only takes a moment for us to watch the news before we're reminded of the dark world. We live in. This darkness seems inescapable it crawls into our government and school systems. Seeps into our entertainment, and captures the vulnerable with false promises of satisfaction, and freedom. And while those who have been enraptured by this darkness. Appear to be relishing in its pleasures the truth is they remain trapped in its bondage. It's often tempting for us to look the other direction to allow the enemy to continue controlling this world. With so much evil lurking around every corner is no wonder. We often prefer to remain shut away safe behind closed doors. This enemy is a spirit. It's everywhere even in your home. When you sit there and just watch. What's on social media all day long. It invades your mind, thoughts, and takes control of you. You are the salt of the Earth. But if the salt loses its saltiness how can it be made salty again? It is no longer good for anything except to be thrown out, and tramped underfoot. You are the light of the world. A town built on a hill cannot be hidden. Neither do people light a lamp, and put it under a bowl. Instead they put it on its stand. And it gives light to everyone in the house in the same way. Let your light shine before other. That they may see your good deeds and glorify your father in heaven. Matthew 5 13-16.

Head Shepherd
P.O.G.
Loving Ministry

Spirit SMALL

"Small minds have small thoughts". Good morning People of God. We are a small insignificant spot in this vast universe that God has created. It seem there always some bigger, or better idea then what we are thinking. We always stop ourselves from thinking big, because we think it is impossible to do. When you have God on your side all things are possible. God has always used small people in the bible to do extraordinary things. He works through them to bring out their greatness. Moses was a man with a speech problem, and a murderer who was on the run from the law. God used him to free his people from bondage. Moses was a small man God gave him power to defeat an Emperor. He can do the same for you just stop thinking your small. Have big dreams, big ideas, and believe in yourself that you can do big things. God can magnify any small things, and make it a great thing. There are no small peoples just small ideas just change the way you look at yourself. There is a giant in you just waiting to be awaken. Arise and take this world by storm. When you think big, big things will happen for you that is the power of the universe. God says what a person think that is who they are, so think big.

Head Shepherd
P.O.G.
Loving Ministry

Spirit
SMILE

Job 9:27 If I say" I will forget my complaint, I will change my expression, and smile.

Good morning people of God. The most healthy thing you can do in life is smile. There has been studies stating that when you are happy you live longer. Why is it so hard for some of us to do this? I know life has been hard on you, and friends are not seeing things your way. But when you keep a positive attitude about things life seems better. There is no team that will win all the time. You will loose in some situations in life. But stay positive about it. We must go through pain to be able to enjoy the good things in life. The enemy is so hard at work to keep you miserable in life. God has promised you happiness when you have the right attitude. Just know that whatever storm you go through in life the calm will be in the morning. Have faith knowing God is there with you. There is no sorrow he cannot protect you from. Smile be happy life is good when you have God on your side. When you make the decision to joyfully and willingly to do what you love, whether as a hobby or career, You help contribute the amount of happiness, and joy that exist in the world. Have you ever notice the rich, and famous are always smiling with a good attitude. To obtain the good things in life be grateful, and appreciate what God has given you already. JUST SMILE.

Head Shepherd
P.O.G.
Loving Ministry

Spirit
SMILE

Job 29:24 When I smiled at them, they scarcely believed it; the light of my face was precious to them.

Good morning people of God. People in society now a days have forgotten how to smile. They walk around with this blank look on their face. No eye contact just looking straight ahead. Thinking about only themselves never noticing the person next to them. A simple smile can change someones day from bad to good. It doesn't cost you anything to give a smile, but it can be priceless to someone. You can change that person mood by letting them know someone care about them. It is so easy to do why not do it. Even you feel good when you are smiling. Happiness have help people overcome their sickness and depression. Smiling is a key to better health. When you smile the whole world will smile back at you. Don't always think a person with a smile on their face is up to something lol. Have you ever notice that people who are wealthy are always smiling? You will attrac positive happy people around you then life will be more enjoyable. A genuine smile involves the muscle affecting the eye, mouth, cheek, and eyebrow, they are hard to feign genuine smile are a response to positive emotions, or can convey things like joy, pleasure, encouragement, and appreciation. Across all cultures people smile so why not smile back, and let them know you care about them.

Head Shepherd
P.O.G.
Loving Ministry

Spirit
SPIRITUALITY

John 16:13 But when he, the Spirit of truth, comes, he will guide you into all the truth. He will not speak on his own; he will speak only what he hears, and he will tell you what is yet to come.

There are over 41000 religions denomination in the world. But there is only one universal God. Why do you think there are so many denomination? It is a tool of the enemy to keep us in darkness and confusion. When you can keep the people divided you are able to control them. God lives in all of us we are part of his DNA. Your soul is a frequency that connect us to God. We need to have a strong foundation of faith let God be your moral, and spiritual compass. The ultimate God loves each Of us as a unique son or daughter. You have to learn to connect to the Christ energy in you. When will we start listening to our heart. Then your are beginning to listen to God We must have free thought, and free will to be who we are in life. The enemy don't want you to have those choices. With wisdom we will know what the enemy is up to. Ask the father to give us the knowledge to know what is right in life. Be the change you want to see in the world. Awareness is the 1st step towards positive change. When we are able to overcome our fear. Then you begin to be in control of your life. Christ power can change all your difficulty of life. Stop rushing thought life and slowdown then the spirit will guide you to paradise.

Head Shepherd
P.O.G.
Loving Ministry

Spirit
STAND OUT

Never give up on a dream just because of the time it will take to achieve it. The time will pass anyway, why do we work so hard to fit in? When we were born to stand out. You can do all kinds of things to be noticed, but many of them don't make a lasting impression. Most entrepreneurs are people of impulse, and most passionate people live by feelings. But those who understand and practice the art of discipline can channel those impulses into something of substance. Get feedback from others and learn as much as you can about how you come across. Then you can accurately target how you appear in a crowd, and what you need to work on. When you truly believe you can create what you envision when you're not afraid of the obstacles. That confidence will automatically make you stand out from the rest. Some people have it, some people don't, but all of us can fake it. We're talking presents were talking charisma, we're talking standing out in a crowd. What is it about these impressive characters that make stop and look when they walk into a room? How do they manage to command attention without even trying? Be good at what you do know who you are, have passion and communicate all this through a carefully balanced blend of physicality, personality, presence and inner confidence. standing out in a crowd is all about mutual respect.

Head Shepherd
P.O.G.
Loving Ministry

Spirit
STAND UP

Leviticus 19:32 Stand up in the presence of the aged, show respect for the elderly and revere your God. I am the Lord.

Good morning people of God. I once heard that if you don't stand for something you will fall for anything. The enemy has made this world so confusing. Legalized marijuana, prostitution, and in some states you can have two wives. It is hard enough already to do what is right. Because so many are doing wrong. Be a person with some character about yourself stand up for what is right in life. Stop being afraid of the enemy and face him down. In our communities there is so much violence, rapes, and murders, and thefts. We know who the perpetrators are we are afraid to tell authorities. Stand UP and Tell Someone! Some of us are in abusive relationships verbally, and physically, we feel we cannot do better for ourselves Stand UP and Leave! We tell our kids to get a job, and not teach them to have a career. Stand UP tell them about higher education, so that they can be somebody in life! We live our lives always worried, and afraid to live a righteous life thinking about what others are saying about us. We are Gods people you should not be afraid or worry about anything. Our God is an awesome God. He parted the red sea so the Israelite could be free. Pharrels army was drowned in the red sea. He healed the sick, made the blind sea, and rouse the dead so that you can be set free. God said he will make your enemy your foot stool. There is power in you so don't be afraid stand up when you see something is wrong. Speak out for justice help your fellow man. In the end we win, because no weapon formed against you shall prosper.

Head Shepherd
P.O.G
Loving Ministry

Spirit
STRENGTH

....

The quality or state of being physically strong. Strive not to be a success, but rather to be of value. If you ask people to share their strength what kind of response do you expect? Silence, probably, hesitation, uncertainty, self consciousness, and when people finally come up with one strength, to every ten weaknesses, they say it like a question. I'm a good listener? Maybe? Why are we so confident about weaknesses, and so uncertain when it comes to our strengths. Its because we tend to focus on the negative when it comes to ourselves, and it when it comes to everybody else too. Its easy to be blinded to your potential when faced with challenging times. But its important to persevere as going through these times is part of the process to fulfilling that potential. If you are not willing to risk the usual you will have to settle for the ordinary. Being strong always come down to this, focus, and effort, and you control both! Isiah 41:10 fear not for i am with you. Be not dismayed, for i am your God i will strengthen you. I will help you I will uphold you with my righteous right hand. Challenging situations, and obstacles are a part of life. When you're faced with one focus on the good things no matter how small, or seemingly insignificant they seem. if you look for it you can always find the Good in it. Even if its not immediately obvious. The person who become stronger is the person who wants it the most.

Head Shepherd
P.O.G.
Loving Ministry

Spirit
STRONG FAITH

Hebrews 11 Now, faith is the substance of things hoped for, the evidence of things not seen. For by it the elders obtained a good report. Through faith we understand that the worlds were framed by the word of God, so that things which are seen were not made of things which do appear.

Good morning people of God. Would you as people of God be willing to stand by God's words without a shadow of doubt. Believing in his words 100 % standfasting with them. There was a king named Darius who made a golden statue for his people who he said was their God.

He said No one is to pray to any other God, but just this golden God. His right hand man Daniel, still prayed to the almighty God three times a day.

The king made a law that if anyone was caught praying to other gods he would put them in the lion's den so that they could be torn apart and eaten by the lion.

Daniel had faith in his god and still prayed to him. Then one day he was busted praying to his God and taken to the king for punishment. The king said, Didn't I tell you to pray only to my god?

Daniel said, "My God is God."

Then you have broken my law. Although you are my boy, I must still punish you. He put Daniel in the lion's den at night so he would not see what was going to happen to him.

Daniel prayed in the den and an angel of the lord tied the lion's mouth so that they could not eat him.

When morning came, the king went to see if Daniel had been eaten by the lions, but he only saw him asleep with them.

Then the king knew Daniel's God was God.

Faith means something different to everyone. For some it's about participating in an organized religion, going to church, synagogue, a mosque and so on.

For others, it's more personal. Some people get in touch with their spiritual side through private prayer, yoga, meditation, quiet reflection, or even long walks.

Though we can't prove the existence of one (or many) Gods, we can provide evidence for the power of faith. For Good or evil, faith factors into every day functioning. We've evolved to believe.

Religion can help us make sense of our world, provide motivation, and bind us together.

Nevertheless, structured belief has its drawbacks. So keep your mind open when dealing with faith.

Even though I walk through the valley of the shadow of death, I will fear no evil, for you are with me.

People of God, you must have faith in something other than man, so believe in him to keep you on the paths of righteousness.

Head Shepherd
POG
Loving Ministry

Spirit SUCCESSION

It is only when we take chances when our lives improve. The initial and most difficult risk that we need to take is to become honest. A number of people or things sharing a specific characteristic, and following one after the other.. We as spiritual beings must teach others, to become leaders in the world. Then there will always be someone to take over our place. The enemy knows if he can take out the head. The world will no longer grow. A good leader needs to know that their behavior will matter a lot To the people they are leading. They will be listening to them, watching them, and they will care deeply what they do.. There are best chance of success is to learn how to act like a leader before they become one. You must break old habits, and form new ones. They need to improve their interpersonal skill, and learn to think strategically, and become effective at influencing others. Effective successor have major impacts on not only the team they manage, but also their company as a whole. People who work under great successor tend to be happier more productive, and more connected to their organization, and this has a ripple effect that reaches your organization's bottom line. Greatness is difficult greatness is defined by how much you want to put into what you do. You know how to fight through the worst day of your life to get to the best days of your life. Comfort is your biggest trap and coming out of your comfort zone is your biggest challenge. Hebrews chapter 13 verse 7 Remember your leader who spoke the word of God to you. Considered the outcome of their way of life and imitate their faith.

Head Shepherd
P.O.G.
Loving Ministry

Spirit
SURRENDER

Good morning people of God. We live our whole lives trying to accomplish our goals, and dreams in life. Never once do we want to give up on them. It seems that we are all alone, and that there is no one who can see what we see. At times the road become difficult there are so many doors being closed on us. People are telling us what we are doing is good. But is not willing to help out with finance. Whenever you are trying to make a difference in life it takes money to change somethings. The enemy has made people hard and cold to others needs. We can see someone hurting, and it does not touch our hearts. There is not a tear or a second thought to try, and help them. What has happen to this world why are they so cold. Its time we turn our lives over to God. Let go and let God guide your life. There is no problem that we can solve there is no problem he cannot heal. God is a positive energy that control the universe he is the beginning, and the end of all things. There is no sorrow or pain he cannot take away. You must have faith, and believe that change is coming. There is an energy in you when you stay positive, and feel good there is God in you. Hornest this energy, and all things can be possible. God says when you believe he will make your enemy your footstool. Just release the controls, let God guide you through this difficult life. You are the head, and not the tail.

Head Shepherd
P.O.G.
Loving Ministry

Spirit

SUSTAINING LOVE

God so loved the world that he gave his only begotten son so that you can have everlasting life. Good morning people of God. Do we as P.O.G. know what sustaining love mean? To love someone unconditionally with out there being some rewards. You should love people for who they are, and not what they have to offer you. Help the sick, homeless, and those in need. We carry the message of loving of acceptance, to those who are discriminated against or forgotten. We feed the hungry ones cloth the naked ones, and comfort those who morn. Powered by the spirit, we shine hope into the lives of those weighed down by sin. This is how Jesus loved when he was here on earth. Your heart must have compassion for humanity. When you put others needs before yours then do what it takes to help others you are beginning to be like Christ. This will be a difficult challenge. Stay filled with faith. God will change your mind and let it be filled with mercy and grace. Believe that this can and will be done. Your life will be changed into something great. You're doing the will of God. Don't be afraid what others will think about you. Always do what is right in life. Yet some will cheat on you, manipulate and use you. People are bitter and distrustful of love. Just leave it up to God to be your judge who will take care of it for you. Be a person of substance this will take some effort. So hold on change is coming.

Head Shepherd
P.O.G.
Loving Ministry

Spirit STRENGTH

Your spiritual strength is much more powerful than your physical strength. The quality or state of being physically strong. If you believe you can, you probably can. If you believe you won't you most assuredly won't. Belief is the ignition switch that gets you off the launching pad. You have to develop your spiritual strength with prayer, meditation, everyday of your life. Because we live in a culture that increasingly leans toward commercialism, materialism, and secularism, it is not easy to keep the soul nourished. The challenge of these days when times are not hospitable to spiritual growth, is how to nurture, feed, heal, restore, and renew the soul. As p.o.g. we are to let blessings flow through us, and on to others to often we go through life oblivious to the good that comes flowing into our lives. Get creative with language, and speak words that will uplift, encourage, hearten, and bless other people. As you build them up your own. Spirit will get stronger. ISAIAH 41:10 fear thou not i am with thee be not dismayed. For i am thy God. I will strengthen thee you, I will help thee you I will uphold thee with the right hand of my righteousness. If you are working on something that you really care about you don't have to be pushed the vision pulls you!

Head Shepherd
P.O.G
Loving Ministry

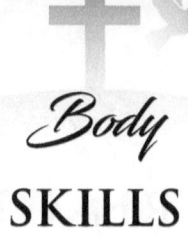

Body SKILLS

Ecclesiastes 2:21 For there is a man whose labor is with wisdom, knowledge, and skill; yet he must leave his heritage to a man who has not labored for it. This also is vanity and great evil.

Even at birth God put a gift in you. Our parents make sure they need to develop that gift. Other customs watch their children and study them to know what they are good at doing. So when they know what it is that they are good at, they put them up with an elder who will train them on that gift so they can blossom.

We in America today need to do this so our kids will know what they are good at as they grow up. We don't want to work with our hands anymore. It seems hard work is something of the past. We need to go back to being a nation of hard workers, so we can make this country great again!

People want to do the less and make the most in their jobs today. Computers have made this a lot easier on people so they can just sit and type on a keyboard all day or just talk for their living.

We need all types of people in the workforce to make this world go around. Let's teach our children a skill again, like: Carpentry to build a house; plumbing or electrical work.

There are a variety of things your child can do. We all can not be a society of doctors and lawyers or presidents. Then who will take care of them?

First we must understand what a skill is. The encyclopedia says what a skill is. A skill is the learned ability to carry out a task with pre-determined results often within a given amount of time, energy, or both.

In other words, the abilities that one possesses. Skills can often be divided into domain-general and domain-specific skills.

For example, in the domain of work, some general skills would include time management, teamwork and leadership, self-motivation and others, whereas domain-specific skills would be useful only for a certain job. Skill usually requires certain environmental stimuli and situations to assess the level of skill being shown and used.

Now that we know what a skill is, let's make sure our children have one. It will take determination and lots of discipline to instill a good skill. But it will be worth it. Once your child has his/her values in place they will be there for them to use whenever needed for survival.

Remember, the Good Book says, "spare the rod, spoil the child." They may hate you now but they will thank you later in life.

Head Shepherd
POG

Spirit
STAND STILL

Habakkuk 3:11 The sun and moon stand still in their courses the flash of your arrows drives them away, the bright light of your lightning-quick spear.

Good morning people of God. We as people of God are so quick to get angry when someone do or say something wrong to us. We are ready to give them a piece of our mind by telling them off. God says stay still keep quiet and let him deal with your enemy. But his words we don't remember when the devils anger takes over our minds. We just want to lash out on the person who made us upset. There are times when you must stand still and not progress the situation to a point that someone will be hurt. Jesus told Peter to put down your sword and let the Roman Guards do their jobs. What if Peter did not do this and the Roman Guards killed them all? Then Gods purpose for Jesus dying on the cross would have never happened. There are times when you need to let go and let God take care of the situation. Standing still in troubling water is hard to do but we must remain calm to stay afloat God has promised when you remain still when all things are blowing up around you he will protect you from any harm. You must have faith and believe in these words to help bring you through the storm. He leads me beside still water he restores my soul I walk through the valley of the shadows of death l fear no evil for you are with me. The lord shall fight for you. You must be still.

Head Shepherd
P.O.G.

Spirit
SAFE HAVEN

Judges 6:23 The Lord said to him", You are safe! Do not be afraid! You are not going to die.

Good morning people of God. Can the faithful among us really feel safe, in the midst of a world going mad and out of control? A world where hurricanes drown innocents and tares' apart homes, a mad man shooting in church, and Vegas killing, and hurting many. Unspeakable violence just a given part of our collective human existence. Life in our fast pace, often impersonal, cold and confusion world may elicit from us the same sort of dialogue with God. People for decades have moved from community to community, state to state looking for a safe place to live. There aren't any more safe places the devil knows where he can cause the most harm. We need to take time to read the bible again and pray these words. We have come to the right place. With God, we can feel safe and happy taking refuge in our loving lord. Until people can stop the hating of one another and try to understand each other the devil will always have the upper hand on us. Think about this? If all people was blind how would we look at life? Without color will we be nicer to each other? We are all made in the image of the almighty God. We are all the same. If you cut us do we not all bleed red? We must come to terms and understand that if we cannot all get along the enemy will win. The killing, hunger, homeless, and hate will consume the world. It's time for the good people to make a stand and start doing what is right again. We must follow his words and commandments with consistency we are in the end times of the unknown anything can happen at any time. You must prepare yourself by praying and reading the bible daily.

Asking our father in heaven, to put his arms around your family and love ones. He will protect you from all harm if you just believe in him. Change the way you look at life know things can and will get better. Fill all your thoughts with goodness, happiness and peace on earth. Our father who is in heaven will keep us safe from the evil one. Just have faith and live your life without worries. Love each other by caring and sharing for one another.

Head Shepherd
P.O.G.
Loving Ministry

Spirit
TIME

Genesis 8:22 While the earth continues to exist, planning time and harvest, coal and heat, summer and winter, and day, and night will not cease:

Good morning people of god. It seems we never have enough time to do the things we need to get done in life. Always rushing through life not knowing when we will finish what we need to get done with. Time is not on anyone side just put things in order and start with what is most important then do that first. Time passes on so quickly we are growing older each and every day. Time is something we have no control over and cannot turn back the hands of time. We are running out of time, it is time for us to prioritize what is important to be doing in life, like putting Christ back in it. We must prepare for the afterlife, God have mercy on our soul. There is so much sorrow and pain in this life, do you want that in your afterlife also .It is time to forgive others for what they have done to you, and loving everyone again starting with yourself first. Time can heal all your pain if you just ask for help from Jesus. Time can be a wonderful if you believe and have faith in the father. Time marches on and so shall we with the following of god's words and his laws. To be ready for a joyful after life try having some joy in your heart. It's time to smile again and not worry about the bad things in life. Leave it all up to Christ and he shall make all things right again. Time is such a mystery that we do not know what will happen at any moment. So it's time for you to turn your life over to Jesus, so your soul can have a good time in the afterlife. It's time to ask for forgiveness, it's time to pray, and time to start loving all humanity. Time is something we do not have enough of so stop procrastinating and have some self control start planning for your afterlife. Whenever you push back what you should be doing, you are increasing the distance once again between you and the finish line. Now more urgent goals will loom and your original goal will linguist in the back of your mind. We need to find ways to shorten the distance between where we are now and where we want to end up..And that is with the heavenly father. Time IS NOT ON ANYONES SIDE

Head Shepherd
POG

Spirit
TARGET

Lamentations 3:12 He drew his bow and made me the target for arrows.

Good morning people of God. P.O.G. we must have some type of target to hit in life. If you are going through life with out a target how would you know when you hit it. A target is a good measure to see if you are on the right track. When you are trying to achieve anything in life you must have a plan of action to obtain it. All companies use a target to hit their objectives. God has a plan in store for your life. He has a target for when it will happen for you. There is so much you can do in life, but you need to stay on course. Figure out what is your gift in life. God has placed something wonderful inside you. Stop going through life aimlessly not knowing your target. How can you hit your target if you don't know what it is? You cannot be like everyone else. There is a specific gift that God has placed in you. Ask for guidance from your heavenly father to help you discover what it is. Write down what your target is. Be very detailed about how you want it to be. Sign and write thank you on it and then put it away, and not look at it again. This is your faith knowing that God will make it happen for you. Believe in yourself and the father then all things will be possible again.

Head Shepherd
P.O.G.
Loving Ministry

Spirit
TRUE FRIEND

Job6:14 Anyone who with holds kindness from a friend forsake the tear of the almighty.

Good morning people of God. We have so many friends in life even on face book there are many. Do you know what a true friend is, and what is a good friendship? A true friend is someone who is there not only in the good times, but bad as well. When the storms of life comes your way a true friend is there holding your hand until the end. They will not criticize you for doing wrong, but give you good advice on how to make it right. A true friend will not talk about you behind your back. But will always uplift you to others. When the storms of life has pass, and you are back, on the road to greatness, and receive your rewards. A true friend will not be envious of you but instead they will help you celebrate your victories. True friend will never hate on you for being a winner in life. They will be happy for you, and share with others how great you are. A true friendship is hard to come by, because we are taught in life to be better than others no matter what is the price. A true friend is someone who will give you unconditional love. But the one friend who will be there for you even in the after life is your heavenly father above. So why not try to befriend him. He will always confirm your friendship with him.

Head Shepherd
P.O.G.
Loving Ministry

Spirit
THE HARD WAY!

Genesis 18:14 Is anything too hard for the lord? I will return to you at the appointed time next year, and Sarah will have a son.

Good morning people of God. Why is it that we as P.O.G. sometimes we want to do things with out asking God about it? It's our way or the highway. We will not listen to anyone's advice. We know what we are doing. Many times we need to stop, and think about what will be the outcome. There are always consequences to what we do in life. Don't be so quick to jump, into something with out thinking it through first. We all need some guidance in life from someone. If someone is willing to give you some good advice, why not take it. To observe that life obtain unavoidable difficulties it is not to minimize it, impacts, or suggest, that we should give up trying to make life better. But people – me included-add a lot of unnecessarily frustration, anxiety, and self criticism, by resisting difficulties- often with an underlining attitude of it shouldn't be this way. Your heavenly father he wants you to have a peaceful, and joyful life. The spirit that dwells in you gives you a direct line of communication to the father. So when times become difficult you can just call on him, and to ask him to give you some guidance through the storms of life. Then you will see everything will be alright.

Head Shepherd
P.O.G.
Loving Ministry

Spirit
THINK

Philippians 4:8 Finally brothers and sisters, whatever is true, whatever is noble, whatever is right, whatever is pure, whatever is lovely, whatever is admirable- if anything is excellent or praiseworthy – think about such things.

Good morning people of God. Do you know as humans we only use one third of our brain power. The brain is a powerful organ it can do many things. God says what a person think it's who a person is, imagine you can think of being anything in life. We stop ourselves from being great, because we do not use our full potential of our mind. There has been studies of people healing themselves by thinking about themselves being well. When you have thoughts of positivity the universe will bring these things around you. When you control your thoughts you control your destiny. Being a great thinker like Einstein, or Confucius, have a vision for your life of being someone of importance. Don't let money be all that you seek, want wisdom, and knowledge. Be a person with integrity, and kindness. Always be hungry for knowledge never stop reading. Your mind is a terrible thing to waste so use it to discover your potential in life. The more you know the more you grow life will be wonderful. Your father promise you all things when you believe in him. We go through life never thinking before we act. If we were to think about something before we act it will keep us out of some trouble. Think your situation through before you act on them, and ask God for some guidance. Be a great thinker, and empower yourself, because with wisdom you will understand life.

Head Shepherd
P.O.G.
Loving Ministry

Spirit
THOUGHTS

Your thoughts will become your reality in life. Colossians chapter 3 verse 2 set your mind on things that are above not on things that are on Earth. Spend time with positive friends, and family members to increased lightly hood that their positive thinking happens will become yours too. It's hard to be negative when everyone around you is so positive. When you encounter problems and difficulties in life don't play the role of the victim. Acknowledge your role in the situation and take responsibility for your behavior. Will you think and talk about what you want, and how to get it you feel happier, and in greater control of your life. When you think about something that makes you happy your brain actually released endorphins which give you a generalized feeling a well being. Positivity doesn't always refer to simply smiling and looking cheerful however positivity is more about one's overall perspective on life and their tendency to focus on all that is good in life. Thoughts become perception, perception becomes reality. After your thoughts alter your reality. Work harder on yourself than you do on your job. Then you will become who you want to be in life.

Head Shepherd
P.O.G.
Loving Ministry

Spirit

TOGETHER

Matthew12:25 Jesus said unto them every kingdom divided against itself is bought to desolation, and every city or house divided against itself shall not stand.

Good morning People of God. There are a lot of groups, and organizations in this world today, but are they really together? Even as individuals we have relationships, and families but yet are we really together? Together means on the same accord to achieve the same vision. The three major religions Catholic, Muslims, and Christians even they are not on the same accord. You can go to anyone of their gathering, and you see only one race of people. God says all people should be on the same accord, and that seeking him, and loving others. I am asking P.O.G. nation are we still practicing these beliefs? Some say that segregation has passed, but I can see in our communities its still there. On one side of town we have Hispanics on the other we have blacks. There are some that have built there own community so that they can isolate themselves from others. When will we start being a society of togetherness, and start doing for one another. God says people that pray together stay together. Why is it the only time people come together is when it is a natural catastrophe, or a terrorist attacks we feel vulnerable, and want to help others in these times. We shore up our emotional defenses, and we empathize with victims, and other people. People of different ethnic groups, races, ages, and socioeconomic levels feel just as we do, and are sense an implicit kinship. This should be the feeling that we should have as P.O.G. all the time, and not let race or social status come into play. We should love our neighbors as our father love you. Stop letting petty things keep us apart, let God inside your heart. Start being compassionate, and understanding of that who are different. The air that we breathe is a life that your father has given you. Meaning we all breathe we are his creation do as he tell us. To love one another, and stop the hate.

Head Shepherd
P.O.G.
Loving Ministry

Spirit
TOLERANCE

Effort only fully releases is reward after a person refuses to quit. The ability of willingness to tolerate something in particular the extents of opinions or behavior that one does not necessary agree with. We have been tolerating what the enemy been telling us for centuries. Even though we know he comes to rob, steal, and destroy. It's time to stop letting people manipulate us in life. Our father has tolerated us for a long time for not believing in him. We need to start 1st by believing in ourselves. Take back what has been stolen from us. You are powerful, you can achieve whatever you want in life. You need to believe in God than your dream will come true. People opinion should not matter, because they don't believe in themselves doesn't mean you shouldn't believe in you. Stop tolerating what others are saying about you, and know that the father cares for you! God will show you who you are a person of greatness someone with all powers to do what you want in life. Just believe you are great you can do all things through Christ. God will never tolerate anyone to treat his children wrong. Let every move that you make be guided by God. He will deliver you to the place you should be in life. Never stopped believing in God because he Is perfect. He will heal you of your pain, and struggles in your life.

Head Shepherd
P.O.G.
Loiving Ministry

Spirit TRANSFORMATION

A thorough or dramatic change in the form or appearance. You don't need anybody's permission to make your goals into your reality! Only discipline ones are purely free in life, and in discipline are slaves to their moods and passions. Everybody needs to be good-nature with a good heart, because in this way, we can solve our own problems as well as those of others, and we can make our human life meaningful. Most people never aim to make big changes in their lives. No matter how stuck they feel, they always think. That's who I am. I was born this way or worse. It's just they way it is. Yet The truth is, your personality, and life are fluid. Things can change. You can change. But it won't happen on its own. You need to let go of who you are, so you can become who you might be. Most people have 2 lives, the lives we live and the life we are capable of living. And even though change always takes time, a few months of dedication and focus can help us fundamentally change Who we are, and how we live. If you want to change your life, you first need to get clear on what your life looks like right now. This will help you find out what exactly you want to change. Ideally you'll take a close look at the different areas of your life you want to change. Health, finances, wealth, career relationships. You can expand these areas depending on what feels important to you, but actually this distinction is great place to start. You must have faith, determination, drive, will power and endurance to keep going each day and everyday. Get up and get going in life you were created to overcome every storm and obstacle.

Head Shepherd
P.O.G.
Loving Ministry

Spirit
TRUTH

John chapter 14:6 I am the way, the truth, and the life. No one comes to the father except through me what truth do you believe men or Christ? We have been believing what man has told us for ages. Never questioned him why. God has a plan for your life all we have to do is follow his words. When you know the truth you are able to make the right decisions in life. There will be clarity and a peace of mind. When you listen with your Christ conscience you will know the truth. The purpose of life is to win the battle between evil and good. Truth is when we know what is right in life the only limits are the ones we place on ourselves. You can move mountains it is no I cannot it is how can I? The truth is you can achieve anything in life with God on your side don't compare yourself to people, of the world but people who believe in Christ learn from Other people's mistakes. The Bible puts it this way everything written is written for our learning. The truth is the enemy does not want you to reach your full potential! But God has given you free will so you can determine whatever lifestyle you choose to live. You will know the truth when you feel it! The enemy doesn't want you to know the truth, because if you did you would know that he has no authority over you. Your pure energy don't be afraid to do what's right with your life.

Head Shepherd
P.O.G.
Loving Ministry

Spirit
TELL SOMEBODY

Genesis 27:8 now then, my son, do exactly what I tell you!

People of the world today do not want to tell others about the good things in life. Like how to get a better price on something, a lower loan, or a better health care plan. They feel that they should keep information to themselves so they can be better than others. Even at work when something new happens some people will not tell you about it? Why it is some people need to feel that they are better than others? Even when people see bad things in life they still will not tell anyone. Tell somebody about things that can make their life better, and stop felling like you are better than them. People of God we should all want to be as one, so tell somebody about what can better their life. We all have something that can help someone to live a better life. Share this information with them so we can all be as one. People of God need one another the world is already against us. There are all kinds of discounts in life that someone does not know about so tell them. Even the biggest thing to tell someone is about Jesus, and some will still not tell someone about him. Tell someone how Jesus died on the cross so that you may have everlasting life. Tell someone how Jesus made the blind see and the lame walk. Tell someone how Jesus fed the hungry. Tell someone that Jesus is the way and the light, and the eternal water of life. Let's be People of excellence and show others that God live within us. Stop being afraid to tell someone what can better their lives. If you can't tell someone about the God things of life then your friend is the devil. Tell someone that Jesus love them.

Head Shepherd
P.O.G.

Spirit
TESTING

Deuteronomy8:19 now if you forget the lord your God at all and follow other gods, worshipping and prostrating yourselves before them, I testify to you today that you will surely be annihilated.

Good morning people of God. We as people of God must start passing the test in life, which are the times of troubles and problems in life. God test us all so that your faith will become stronger. The spirit sent Jesus into the desert for his test in time. Who are we to think that we should not have to go through a time of testing? Just pass the test by not getting mad and hurting someone. You must never give up . on God at your time of testing. He is there with you making your faith stronger so you can defeat the devil. A calm mind in a raging storm or on the battle field will always bring you safely through it. Life is full of challenge, disappointment and setbacks. We must believe that this shall pass also. The book of Job is about a man who stood by Gods word no matter what happened in life to him. So, Satan wants God to test Job's faith, because according to Satan, Job's riches can be attributed only to the fact that Job's been blessed with prosperity. According to Satan Job's a good servant of God because his faith has never been tested. God grants Satan permission to test Job's righteousness. Job refuses to forsake his belief in God, and never once cures God. Stay positive when things start going wrong in life. When we were in school we had to study to pass the test, also we must read the bible to know how to pass the test the spirit will give you in life. Remember you are clay still in the fire being shaped. When God is through with you. You shall come forth as pure gold.

Head Shepherd
P.O.G.

Spirit

THANKFULNESS

Colossians 2:7 Rooted and built up in him firm in your faith as you were taught, and overflowing with thankfulness.

Good morning people of God We as people of God must start being more thankful when others do something to help us out. We should appreciate it when someone is offering to help us out in a time of need. We must thank people for the small things that they do for us not just the big stuff. Have a attitude of gratefulness always ready to say thank you. When people know that you are thankful for them helping you out. They will be more willing to help others also. Your family and your kids should be trained in this way also. When the time comes they need someone to help them out it will be no problem for them because they already a person of thankfulness. We as people are always wondering why God does not give us more in life, if we were to be just thankful, for the little things he has given us already then he may give us more. Be thankful for your sight, speech, mobility and health. God words are the truth if you are thankful and grateful he will always have more blessings for you. A thankful heart and a loving spirit will never want but always have in life. Be thankful for Jesus that he gave his life so you may have everlasting life. Thankfulness can be seen across human cultural groups, and it seem to have the evolutionary function of helping people stay deliberately cultivate gratitude, and can increase our well being and happiness by doing so . In addition is associated with increase energy, optimism, and empathy. Remember being thankful is heart healthy.

Head Shepherd
P.O.G.

Spirit
THE SPIRIT OF SELF DOUBT

Job 12:2 Doubtless you are the only people who matter, and wisdom will die with you.

Good morning people of god. Today people are so quick to second guess themselves. Not willing to believe in God or themselves. I believe it is because most of the time fear sets in and stops us from moving forward. This life will always be filled with disappointments it's up to us on how we let it affect us. We should be able to stand strong in Gods words and not be deterred from our dreams. We listen to others telling us we cannot achieve our dreams. That is because they cannot see themselves doing what you are trying to obtain.

People in your inner circle should be people who will up lift you, and not put you down. Life is hard already so, have people around you that are in your corner. Doubt is just the enemy telling you that you cannot have something. That God has already promised you. Believe that God will always take care of his children. He isn't a dead beat dad he loves you. Stop selling yourself short, and know that you are a winner. When you have positive thoughts positive things will happen for you. Change your mind set and change your life. There isn't nothing you can't have in life. If a black man or a crazy man can be president. There isn't nothing impossible for you to achieve in life. Just stop being a doubting Thomas and start being who God created you to be. A person of excellence each and every day. Stop letting the enemy make you feel lesser than the person who God made you to be. You are in control of whatever you put in your mind, and know that whatever you think than that's what it will be. Stay focus on your goal in life. Don't let anyone tell you that you cannot do this. A bit of doubt can be motivating. The excesses are the problem where you doubt yourself, second guess yourself, hesitate, and down yourself. Excessive self doubting negatively affects your judgment, and decisions. You must believe in order to receive anything in life. Tell yourself I will, I can, I must then all things will be possible.

Head Shepherd
P.O.G.
Loving Ministry

Spirit

UNFORGETTABLE

There is a great impact if you focus on what you want to do. Fix your eyes where you want to go. You meet a lot of people over the course of the year. How many of them really remember you? Through not just your name, but who you are on a deeper and more meaningful level? If your only goal is to be known for professional reasons. You're missing out. People who are memorable for the right reason also lived richer, fuller, and more satisfying lives. That's the reason enough to make a few changes in your life. Be a person who encourages motivating, and uplifting others. Be that teacher that beacon of hope, let your light shine the way for others to know what's right in life. Give hope to those who have given up on Christ. Be that person when you walk in the room. Everyone eyes light up and a smile is on their face. In the journey of life we always remember some beautiful places we visited some happy incidents, and some people we met. Why we remember such people, such places, and such incidents. Because there is something special in them which impress our mind. We remember some great leaders, and successful people who we never met, but we only heard about them. Through reading or from studies. If you want others to remember you you must remember them. If you are a busy person meeting many people in A-day you may not be able to remember all about them. But at least you can try to remember. The names of the others. When people come to you and talk about their problems pay attention to what they are talking, and listen to them patiently. When you're able to show concern for a person situation. It makes you unforgettable to them.

Head Shepherd
P.O.G.
Loving Ministry

Spirit
UNIQUE

Isaiah 12:4 at that time you will say: Praise the Lord! Ask him for help! Publicize his mighty acts among the nations! Make it known that he is unique!

Good morning people of God. You are a child of God made in a unique way; no one has your finger prints. There are over 6 billion people in the world and no one has the same finger print. God made you for a purpose. You are unique in your own way. You are a work of art; only one is made that is you. Meaning that God knows you can do something that no one else can. You are a work in progress God is not finished with you yet. He has a lot more in stored for you to accomplish. Just keep the faith and ask what more he has for you to do and he will show you. There is something you can do better than anyone else, you are masterpiece only one made. Believe in yourself take that step of faith and go out into the world and make your life better. You have the same power as the heavenly father does. You can do all things through Christ if you would just try,. God wants to take care of his children, so believe in his words And achieve the things in life you need.

Head Shepherd
P.O.G.

Spirit
VALUE OF LIFE!

Laugh when you can smile everyday. Keep moving forward and don't look back, because life goes by fast, and it only happens once. Finding purpose in life is one of those things that most people want. Whether we know it or not as nice as it sounds, it can seem challenging to attain. This personal sense of purpose guides and sustain you. Day to day and through the years. Even when you have setbacks and the world turns upside down. Purpose gives you stability and a sense of direction. That's why finding purposes is essential for living a happy, healthy life. Because, so much of taking care of our future actually comes from taking a look at our past. We can find many of the answers to where is my life going in the stories of where we've already been. So the best thing you can do if you are feeling loss is to examine areas of your life that are core to helping you reset your directions while be you! Sounds like a cheery poster in a kid's class room. It's actually imperative that you figure out what that means for you because so often we're trying to fit the mode of what we think we should be, but, consider molds they're cold hard limits that make us less of who we really are and the easiest way to get lost is by blending in. If you're not actively coming back to yourself to who you really are in all of your desires, and quirks, and dreams, and traits, the right opportunities and people can't find you. Every champion was once a contender. Who refused to give up!

Head Shepherd
P.O.G.
Loving Ministry

Spirit VIBRATIONS

Proverbs 27:1 Do not boast about tomorrow, for you do not know what a day may bring.

It's time to stop living in doom and gloom environment. We need to change the vibrations of the world. This enemy has already lost, because God has given us the rule of the land. Reclaim your joy, happiness, and knowing that this shall pass. You have endured enough of darkness in your life. It's time to put The Light Of Hope back into your life. Knowing that the almighty God is coming soon to eradicate the darkness in the world. Take the sound of defeat out of your voice. Start giving praise to God again. This is over because, no weapon formed against us shall ever prosper. P.O.G We are the champions of the world because, we are the chosen ones. Be bold, and courageous, and take back the throne which has been stolen. We are heirs to the throne of the universal God. There is nothing we cannot do when we come together, and speak out as one. Say stop the madness I rebuke you, and send you back to hell where you came from. We are Warriors for Christ. Let's take the vibrations way up with love, and hope, to conquer this evil one. When you feel the atmosphere with good cheer. The Lord will surely hear, and send forth his angels to destroy all of your fears. We must stop letting enemy drain us of our energy. This world is a great place when you are able to keep your joy in any situation. Keep your frequency on positivity and live your life to the full.

Head Shepherd
P.O.G.
Loving Ministry

Spirit VICTORIOUS!

Having won a victory triumphant. No matter what the ingredients look like you have to follow the recipe in order to bake the cake. No matter what the trial looked like, you have to follow God's commandments for them to work for your good. Knowing is not enough, we must apply, willing is not enough, we must do the only thing that's important for survival is to adapt, and overcome. Doesn't. matter how strong you are, or intelligent, evolution depends on an adaption, and overcoming a problem. That's the survival of all living things adapt and overcome. That survival The happiest people don't have the best of everything, they make the best of everything. Learn to trust your own thoughts, and breathe, find peace with being alone. Everyone is scared of failure, scared of judgment, scared of the unknown, but there is something for more scarier than that not reaching your full potential in this life that you're capable of, know what your whole mind is thinking, and be completely present in the moment. For most of us the enemy has succeeded in our life. When it comes to self control. You know is no longer working. You can do anything at any time without being restricted by the spirit of God. If the enemy is exercising authority over. Any area of your life please don't give up, always remember, you don't live in the realm of defeat, but in the realm of the victory. You may be down today but it's not over. For a righteous person May fall 7 times and rise again but the wicked shall fall by calamity.

Head Shepherd
P.O.G.
Loving Ministry

Spirit
VOICE

Exodus 4:16 He will speak to the people for you, and it will be as if he were your mouth and as if you were God to him.

God has given us all the voice to speak out against all the injustice in the world. Why is it that so many are afraid to make a stand for what is right in life. God did not give you a spirit of fear. He gave you courage to defeat all the evil in the world. You're voice has power when you use it to stop all the violence in the world. Pay attention to those who are telling you what is right. But in the dark they are doing wrong. When we live our lives with integrity it means that we're always honest, and we let our actions speak for who we are, and what we believe in. It means to tell the truth as you know it, and don't hold back even when your words and your actions may harm another. Stop letting the evil one get away with doing harm to humanity. Let your words be your sword to strike down all the injustice in this world. When we use our our voice as one we create unity. That is sent out to heaven. Make a difference and do what is right in life so the world will be better.. Once you decide your life purpose, you will only have to pick one thing. Your heart! It's easy to give weight to the negative voices that dwell inside each of us. What's difficult is learning to direct kindness towards ourselves, and acknowledge thoughts and feelings without judgment. The world is filled with so many different languages wouldn't it be amazing if we could all speak as one? Your voice is a powerful weapon that can change the perception of life.

Head Shepherd
P.O.G.
Loving Ministry

Spirit
WAKE UP!

Ephesians 6:12 For we wrestle not against flesh and blood, but against principalities, against power, against the rulers of the darkness of this world, against spiritual wickedness in high places.

We tend to go through life in a routine mode. Living life as it comes our way. Not focusing on anything of importance just existing day after day. Doing the same old routine not often do we change it up. Unaware of what is going on around us. The powers to be are passing laws, and legislation to benefit themselves and the rich. Slowly taking away benefits from the poor, and elderly each and everyday. You should know about the people you put in office agenda's before you put them there. When will we start to use our minds to educate ourselves on current affairs. The elite is aware that we don't like to read or be informed. God says knowledge is the key to have a good life. We P.O.G. must have a voice in this world, and not stay asleep. Letting the enemy run this world. I know you feel hopeless saying what can I do, but when we stand as one the enemy will take notice, and treat us with some dignity, and respect. Through out history it took people to unite as one to stop the enemy. So rise and wake up. Start noticing what is going on in society today. The enemy has been hard at work. There is so much we need to change. Lets start by treating each other, and everyone with some love, and respect then we will be able to defeat the dark side.

Head Shepherd
P.O.G.
Loving Ministry

Spirit
WALK YOUR TALK

Focus on what you want in life. You're in control, just go after it, and let God lead you. Keep fighting and be kind to others. Hold your head up high and know that no matter what you're going through, there is always a way. Everyday is a battle. We don't know our last day on this Earth, every day is an opportunity. Be who you were created to be. God is placed something inside of you. That no one can stop. Do what you said and just be you! We tend to get in your own way. After a while of letting ourselves down, we stop taking ourselves seriously. There's only so many times that you can press that snooze button, while firmly swearing that you will wake up, before you stop believing that you successfully will call it quits. You don't even buy it when you say it. We can only disappoint ourselves so much before we stop believing in our world, and we start losing our confidence, and our ability to do what we say. We're going to do. We have to find a way to commit to ourselves, because if we don't, we'll all be serving someone else agenda on someone else timeline. An hour's self-worth will be squashed, because we don't take ourselves seriously. so here is the simplest way to rebuild yourself. Commitment start making small commitments to yourself, and hold to them like it's important to you as though you're running for a president election. We're never going to be 100% of self commitment, and following through on what we say. We're going to do, because that's life. but we sure as heck can improve our record of how we show up with ourselves, because we all want to be our most confident capable selves, and that only happens when we decide that we're worth prioritizing. Get-up-and-get it done. We got this!

Head Shepherd
P.O.G.
Loving Ministry

Spirit WARRIOR

....

We are soldiers and we are on a battlefield in this life. Warriors fight for victory, and freedom with Christ. The Warriors spirit is their greatest weapon. A Warrior knows their spirit is the force that propels them warrior towards their mission. Within the Warrior spirit lies the power that is beyond the flesh, transcending the mental and physical. Spirit is the animating life force that is embedded in all living beings. The Warrior know how to connect with their inner spirit to gang guidance, life force, and power. Darkness cannot drive out the darkness only light can do that. Hate cannot drive out hate only love can do that. Most of us want to be happy, conscious and a source of positivity in the world. But living in these dark these times dominated by materialism, prejudice, and violence, with negative news can make us feel overwhelmed, angry, and hopeless. Whether you pray meditate or practice yoga its impossible to be spiritually victorious without connecting to a higher power to become spiritually powerful practice exercising temperance with your emotions making them your slave instead of your master. Ephesians chapter 6 verse 11 put on the whole armor of God, that you may be able to stand against the schemes of the devil. You have amazing power inside you all you have to do to is unleash it!

Head Shepherd
P.O.G.
Loving Ministry

Spirit WHAT ABOUT

1 Kings 8:45 Then from heaven their prayer and their plea, and uphold their causes.

Good morning people of God We as P.O.G. are always asking God for more things, and not being satisfied with the things we have already. Its like we have a Christmas list year around asking for something. Not once telling your father you are grateful for what he has given you already. We have a home, food on the table, and our children is healthy. He has done so much for us already so try to remember this. When you ask your heavenly father to help others needs then your needs will be meant. What about asking our father to stop the school shootings of our children in the world. Feed the hungry, and make medicare affordable for the elderly, Racial violence against one another. What about just wanting peace here on earth. Life is filled with blessings your father has already given you. You may not see this yet, but his arms are around you to protect you from harm. Worldly possessions will always be here. But when you seek love for others that is priceless. Your father wants you to be Kings, Queens over your home. There is nothing he wont do for you when you love his son Jesus, and others that is your purpose in life. Just ask in the name of Jesus,and it will be done. Believe it deep down inside with all your heart. .There is so much we can ask our heavenly father for. Just start thinking about other people's needs first. Jesus said when you pray the Lords prayer the father will always answer your prayer when you believe.

Head Shepherd
P.O.G
Loving Ministry

Spirit

WHAT YOU DESIRE

Its never too late to become who you could've been. The why truly is the important question. The why gives you a purpose. Why am I doing this? Why does this matter? We must find our purpose in life or else we'll wonder around in circles forever. What is your passion? What are your talents? What are the needs in your community? If you take the time to listen to your inner voice, and trust in yourself, you can rise above self doubt and the judgment of others to truly be able to pursue the goal of having everything you want in life, you need to have an incredibly vivid, and detailed vision for what you want in all aspects of your life. Once you begin to have a clear vision for what you want in your life, then you can truly start thinking about how to achieve everything you want in life. The trouble with not having a goal is that you can spend your running up, and down the field and never score. So not only do you have to understand what it is you want you need to prioritize what you want and understand where things fall in the hierarchy. People need to find what makes them happy in order to full fill their lives. Happiness is truly what we're all after, why do so few people attain it. We have the wrong mindset. We tend to unconsciously define our happiness by what we do, and what we have. The problem is that things we attain are fleeting and the joy they bring quickly subsides. Life is about making an impact, and we need to figure out what we want our legacy to be then start working on leaving that legacy.

Head Shepherd
P.O.G.
Loving Ministry

Spirit

WHAT YOU DO WITH YOUR TIME?

Ecclesiastes 3 A Time for everything. There is time for everything, and a season for every activity under the heavens: a time to be born and a time to die, a time to plant and a time to uproot, a time to kill and a time to heal, a time to tear down and a time to build….

You can tell what a person will be in life just look at how they spend their time. We have been given 24 hours A-day to do what we need to do. Time is more important than money so use it wisely. Time isn't a commodity that you can trade on the stock exchange its priceless. Once it's gone you cannot get it back. It's time to start using it to create the future you want. Stop wasting time doing insignificant things. You must use every moment dreaming of doing the impossible. When you spend your time caring for others they will be time well sent. When you spend your time helping humanity the universe will reward you for that time spent. You must live in the time of the universe,and that is the present time. man made the clock, calendar to keep you stressed and worry. Have you chasing a future goal, and all you have to do is live in the now to create your goal. There's no past or future just now so enjoy your life. When your able to appreciate life in the in the now. The world seems to be a much calmer place. Life is filled with happiness when you look at it differently. Don't put too much pressure on yourself trying to be perfect. Live every moment to the full. Then you will be truly living.

Head Shepherd
P.O.G
Loving Ministry

Spirit
WHO AM I

Exodus 3:14 God said to Moses "I am who I am. This what you say to the Israelite's: I'am has sent me to you.

Good morning people of God. Who are you? Why is it that people spend their whole lives not knowing who they are? Just ask someone that, and see they will have to stop, and think about it. Some will tell you they are a driver, or teache,r or a sales person that's not who they are. That's what they do. You're job title title does not define you in who you were created to be because, some hate what they do. Your heavenly father has placed a gift, and a purpose for you in life when you were in your mothers womb. It is up to us to define, and develop those talents that is with in us. You may ask how will I do this? There is something with in you that you do better than someone else. Just ask those who are close. They will tell you anything that you do. If there is a since of joy in doing it. That is a start on who you really are. Many of us waste our entire life doing things that we really don't like never taking the time to cultivate the gift with in us. You do not need a P.H.D. on who God created you to be. Just call on your heavenly father, and ask him to help you figure out who you are. When you really know you're purpose in life they're will be so much joy in your life, because when you are doing something that you love. Life is then worth living. Just love yourself then love others then you will be on your way being who God created you to be.

Head Shepherd
P.O.G.
Loving Ministry

Spirit

WILLING TO ACT

There are so many times you tell yourself and others that we are going to do something in life. But alone the way we stop doing what we say. Life distractions seem to always take us off our own path. We begin to believe in a negative thoughts in our head. You need a spirit of action do as you say! Don't let someones opinion stop you from accomplishing what you wanted for your life. Take control of your thoughts, and stop limiting yourself. To do what you want for your life. Call to action the spiritual Warrior to fight this darkness surround in your life. If you want to achieve your goals you need to ship from dreaming and to doing. Taking action means laying out a plan to achieve your goals, and putting in a consistent effort to achieve them. Over time you can make the vision of your dreams real. When your goals are too vague you'll have a difficult time making them happen. Getting a clear picture of your goals will eliminate the path forward. Your life would be better if you took the action you've been avoiding. Once you set your goal Striving for success is vital. They're maybe set back alone the way. Don't Wish it we're easier Wish you were better. Always bear in mind that your own resolution to success is more important than any other one thing. Faith without action is dead. The Bible says. When you ready to take command of your life. You must believe in something greater than man. Once you start to believe in yourself there's nothing in the universe you can't have.

Head Shepherd
P.O.G.
Loving ministry

Spirit
WINNING

....

1 Corinthians 15:57 But thanks be to God! He gives us the victory through our Lord Jesus Christ.

Use your voice for kindness your ears for compassion, your hands for charity, your mind for truth, and your heart for love. These are the characteristics of a winner whenever you are able to put others before yourself. That's when you are being who you were created to be. We have been taught to look at winning in a selfish way. This is why the world is in the condition it is today. We should look at it this way when you win we all win. We must learn to fight together no matter what the circumstances stand. We must learn how to think about winning together. We must stop giving up so easily when life start getting hard. We all have gone through hard times, But in the end God brought us through. We must have the attitude of we are going to win. This will not be the end for us. We have to prepare ourselves for winning by believing in God's words. Practice each and every day by living your life the righteous way. When we live our lives as a family for Christ We will be victorious in life. Do not have a lack of faith. We must know we will win. Honor God and believe in him. You were created to do something great. You have so much potential stop having limited beliefs in yourself. Reprogram yourself and how you see life, because life can be whatever you want it to be. Have high positive expectations for your life. The greatest blessing is the mind. We can create whatever reality we choose. Be a winner with God by helping humanity become heaven on Earth!

Head Shepherd
P.O.G.
Loving Ministry

Spirit
WISDOM

James1:5 But if anyone is deficient in wisdom, he should as God, who gives to all generously and without reprimand, and it will be given to him.

Good morning people of God. As the New Year is here, many of us focus our thoughts and prayers on our hopes and dreams for the New Year. Some of these hopes and dreams are personal, but more often than not, they also are for people we care about. We pray for their health, work, relationship, and safety. When I look at the turmoil in the world, both home and abroad, there is plenty of reason to be afraid. We want to trust that our leaders know what they are doing, but we know our human nature well enough to question their judgment. We know and hope that wisdom exists in a world. When the world is in crisis, we long for the wises people to be at the table. We cannot all be Solomon like in our wisdom. Rarely it seems are any of our world leaders the wises in their lands what they can do is make sure that there are, ad least smart enough to surround themselves with wisdom and recognize it when it speak. In the face of injustice, troubles, needs, illness and addiction, victory maybe just the thing for which to pray after all. May God keep us steadfast in the face of adversities?

Head Shepherd
P.O.G.

Spirit
WHY

....

Genesis 44:7 they answered him, "Why does my lord say such things? Far be it from your servants to do such a thing!

Good morning people of God. Why must we as people of God need to know why, things happen to us in life? We are always thinking about the reason why something bad happened to us. "Always asking God why this happen". We need to know about everything in our life, and why things are the way there are. Not once believing in God, and walking in faith, and leaving things in Gods hand. Even when Jesus was here on earth people wanted to know why he was here asking him to prove it to them that he was the son of God. Why can't we just believe in the good things in life, by showing love to one another? Do you really want to know about everything that happens in life? Would it make you more afraid? Or a deeper believer. God says he will protect you from all harm if you just believe in his son Jesus. Why is the sky blue, ocean deep blue, and a sunset so breathtaking? There are some things you don't need answers to just know the father has control over them. If you were to meditate on his words and get control over your thoughts and have holy ones. Then God will reveal some of the wise in life to you. The past cannot be fixed. It can only be healed and learned from. This is why I make a concrete effort, when I am not happy with what someone did, to make it explicit that I am not angry about what happened, only trying to turn it to an opportunity to learn. The big trouble for me is just awareness I am about to ask a "Why questions, and then the transformation of language happens almost by its self. Instead of the habitual "I want to know why you did what you did. I remind myself that what was done has already happened. I might need to mourn it in order to have some acceptance. Whatever I do in the end I cannot change the fact that what this person did is done. I can only focus on now and the future, and say so in so many words, such as "I want to learn from what happen to support smother operation in the future.

Head Shepherd
P.O.G.

Spirit
WAITING

....

Psalm 31:24 be strong and confident, all you who wait on the lord!

Good morning people of God. People in life always seem to be waiting on one thing or another. Everyone has their own thing they are waiting for. It can be a better job, or a better relationship. We all are waiting on some kind of happiness in life. The time we spend thinking about that thing we are waiting to happen in life. We could have made it happen already. Risk keeps us at a standstill in life not willing to make any effort to go forth what we want. Hoping all the time that this thing we are waiting for will come our way soon. Then once we have it the cycle begins all over again. Waiting on the next big thing in life to happen for us. Waiting on something is a big part of our life. You wait to see the doctor, waiting on the bus, and we even spend some time waiting in a line. Why is it that we are willing to wait so patiently for what we want in life? We spend our entire life waiting on something, but the one thing we should be waiting on is the return of Christ. On this day we should all be filled with mercy and grace. There will be no more pain or worry but just happiness and peace. Christ will change the bad things in the world, and there will be only joy and laughter. People will love one another again and be willing to help each other out. There will be no more Racism just everyone living in harmony. This is something worth waiting for. One day, every knee will bow before God and worship Christ. All people of the earth will praise God. That will be a joy filled day, and we await it with longing, and anticipation. We can praise the lord,and serve our neighbors today; knowing that one day all the world will join us. We have all become use to speedier delivery of all services, and when frustration by delay we express our anger openly, and vehemently. And it is getting much worst as our expectations of immediate gratifications are growing. Just be patient God is coming.

Head Shepherd
P.O.G.
Loving Ministry

Spirit
WHAT IF

Isaiah 42:4 He will not grow dim or be crushed before establishing justice on the earth; the coastlands will wait in anticipation for his decrees.

Good morning people of God. People in life today are always saying what if 'I have done this". Why is it we think like this. Never wanting to try and make things happen for us? What if is just another saying to stop you from God glory? We wait all our lives on this day, when everything will be alright to do this thing we want to do in life. There will never be a perfect time to do something you want to do in life. Just do it. Walk out on faith and let God show you how. What if you will never know if you don't try to achieve the good things in life? You have great potentials in you. We are made in God's image with the ability to do all things in Christ. Believe in yourself know that you are capable of doing whatever you want in life. Have a mind set of positivity. Drawing in all the good things in the universe drawn to you. What if our heavenly father will return today? Will you be ready? Stop what if and start doing the things that are right in life. Loving one another. Sharing with one another, and caring about each other. These are the things that our father would like to see when he returns and say unto you. Well done my faithful servants.

Head Shepherd
P.O.G.
Loving Ministry

Visit us on People of God Loving ministry @ weebly.com for your donations

Spirit

WHO HAS SAY OVER YOUR LIFE?

Job 9:16 if I summoned him, and he answered me, I would not believe that he would be listening to my voice.

Good morning people of God We as people have given controls over to others so that they can speak what will happen to you in life. Your mate tells you that you are a loser and you believe them. Your parents tell you that you will never amount to anything in life you believe them. Even the doctors tell you that you have six months to live you believe that also. At what point did we stop believing in the father and ourselves? There is power in you. That the heavenly father has given you. Your mind will determine your outcome in life. If you just think and believe it will be alright then it will be. Stop letting people tell you bad things about yourself, and you stop believing them also. You must always have positive thoughts and a good outlook on life. God is in control, and he knows what is good for you. Stop letting the devil distort your thoughts and feeling your head with evil. The devil is afraid of P.O.G. he knows God has our back. That is why he is causing so much wrong in the world today. Stop letting others speak things over your life. Believe in his words not others. God's words are filled with power and healing. Those are the things you should be saying about yourself and others. We as P.O.G. must pray for others and ourselves for protection from the devil. Then God will put his shield around your family and friends. There is power in many, and not in one. We must stand together, and be a voice of hope. Let the enemy know we will not be defeated. Even if you can't touch or see someone you feel connected if you hear their voice. Listening enhance the health of your marriage and other close relationships. Listening to yourself enables you to live with –well being, especially if you combined listening to yourself with listening to others. Listening to your body keeps you physically healthy. In between a couple listening is an act of love. Listen to God and all things will be possible. THERE IS POWER IN THE WORD!

Head Shepherd
P.O.G.
Loving Ministry

Spirit
WHO AM I

Exodus 3:14 I am who I am. This is what you are to say to the Israelites, I am has sent me to you".

Good morning people of God. People today in the world do not know who they really are. They spent their time trying to be like someone else. Not knowing what their true gift are in life. We go around imitating others trying to fit in and trying to be like them. Even the people we hang around with don't know who we really are, because your playing a game of masquerade with them. Scared and afraid to let them know the real you. God created you in his own image you are a person of importance. Stop feeling like you're not worthy of love in life. Believe and know you have great powers in you. You must tap into your mind and create reality for yourself. You're capable of doing all things just believe this. Speak it over your life and start believing in it. You are a conqueror you are in complete control over your destiny. Have faith and be encourage to live your life. Be who God made you to be kings, and queens over your domain.

There is greatness in you start believing this, and create something wonderful in your life. Your mind and thoughts can visualize what you want to do in life don't be afraid to go after it. Action is something you must take to achieve anything good in life. Find your true self know who you are that is a child of God. Know with out a shadow of doubt you are a winner. Things will happen for you when you speak it over your life. Imagine yourself to be your own boss coming and going as you please. No time clock to punch, and no one telling you what to do.

You have this capability to make your life as you visualize it. Just believe in your father and yourself. Then you will know you are who God says you are a conqueror.

Head Shepherd
P.O.G.
Loving Ministry

Spirit
WELL DONE

Matthew 25:21 His lord said to him, "Well done, good and faithful servant. You have been faithful over a few things, I will set you over many things. Enter into the joy of your Lord."

Good morning People of God. On this holiday season let's be people of well done. Share and help out one another where needed. Buy some groceries and give them to a family for food. It could be someone in your family. Just do it and see how happy they will be.

Have someone pay their rent so they won't be put out in the cold or let them stay with you for a little while.

Homeless people need warm clothes to wear. Buy them a coat, gloves, and a hat to keep them warm.

Go visit that person in the hospital and the ones incarcerated to show them someone still cares about them.

There are so many things we can do as People of God to help out each other.

Think about when you were in need of help and someone helped you out, it was wonderful right?

Be a good servant of god and be about helping the lesser of thee. When you do this your needs will always be met. Jesus fed a multitude of people with just two loaves of bread and two fish. We can just feed one.

Let this be a season of starting a new tradition of giving and sharing with one another so we can change our children's future so they will learn the message of giving and sharing, and not be a world of selfish people of god.

We all need some help in one way or another. So give, so someone may give back to you. These are god's laws. What you do unto others will be done unto you. Why sit around waiting on the miracle to come when you can be one who brings miracles to others.

So on the day of judgment God will say WELL DONE my faithful servants.

Head Shepherd
POG

Spirit
WHAT YOU CARE ABOUT?

Jeremiah 12:2 you plant them like trees and they put down their roots. They grow prosperous and are very fruitful. They always talk about you. But they really care nothing about you.

Good morning people of God. There is so much chaos in the world today natural disasters, terrorist, and mass killings. Families are not spending times together anymore like the old days. People are walking around with the look of uncertainty on their face. The love for others has grown so small. It's easier to hate one another than to love. Why have we as people turned to a cold society. We are only concerned about ourselves. You quickly dismissed your sons, and daughters when they have a problem. What do you care about? Life has a purpose for all of us. There must be compassion in your heart for humanity. Being willing to help your family, and friends when they need you to. Then just maybe you can help someone you don't know. We are only concerned about money, wealth, and possessions in life. The devil has brain washed us along with the media making us believe these are the things we must seek. The world is filled with people who want these things. But we as P.O.G. must know what our real purpose is on earth. That is to be caring and sharing with one another. Wanting to stop the killing, homelessness and hunger in the world. People loving each other as Christ love you. We have to show others how the world should be if we all knew Christ. What you should care about is family and friends. Starting with your family first. You should want to help one another in any way possible. We are so quick to flee from home when we think we are grown. Not willing to stay together and help build family wealth. Then we would of have things in life if we just stayed and prayed together. Why we just can't all get along.

Head Shepherd
P.O.G.
Loving Ministry

Spirit
WARRIORS FOR GOD

Ephesians 6:11-13 Good Morning People of God!

We as people of God must make a decision to be warriors for God. Stop letting society dictate to us what we should do or say in life. Stand up for what is right. Have a backbone. Be a man or be a woman with courage running through your veins. Have a heart to stop the suffering and the hunger in the world. Speak out when you see something that isn't right.

Stop being on the sidelines and get in the game with Christ!!! We are people of the most high with resurrection blood in us.

Take action for Christ when you know things aren't right. We are not cowards, but warriors of Christ fighting a spiritual warfare with the Devil. So put on God's whole armor (the armor of a heavy-armed soldier which God supplies), that you may be able successfully to stand up against (all) the strategies and the deceits of the Devil.

For we are not wrestling with flesh and blood (contending only with physical opponents), but against the despotisms, against the powers, against (the master spirits who are) the world rulers of this present darkness, against the spirit forces of wickedness in the heavenly (supernatural) sphere.

Therefore put on God's complete armor, that you may able to resist and stand your ground on the evil day (of danger), and, having done all (the crisis demands), to stand (firmly in your place).

Let's fight the good fight of faith. We are victors not victims. IN THE END, WE WIN!!!!

Head Shepherd
POG

Spirit
YOUR MUST

> Genesis 4:7 If you do what is right, will you not be accepted? But if you do not do what is right, sin is crouching at your door: it desires to have you, but you must rule over it.

There are things you must in consider on doing in life. If you want to have a wonderful life. You need to start loving yourself, and people around you, because when you love someone that love will come back. Peace of mind is something you need to maintain in all situations. This world is starting to change dramatically! We all need to learn how to remain calm in the storm. There will be times when you need to be calm. When your perception of life is positive that is a sign that something is driving you other than man. You must know your heavenly father is always there with you when you're feeling low. Be encouraged he will uplift you, and put you on the cloud of high. We are all his children there is nothing he would not do to take care of our difficulties. Even though you're walk in life may get weary. He will give you the strength to carry on. Be not deceived God is Not mocked whatsoever a man soweth that shall he also reap. Be of good cheer loving, caring, and sharing, with each other. Your mind is a powerful thing whatever you program it to think. That shall it be, so think of goodness, mercy, and Grace. These are the things your father wants you to meditate upon to make Humanity a place of peace. You must pray, and have a pure mind. Let the Lord guide you through the trials of Life. Be thankful, grateful for what everything in life, and appreciate everyone around who help you in life. When you do these must the universe will change for you everything will turn out for the good in life.

Head Shepherd
P.O.G.
Loving Ministry

Spirit
YOUR SOUL

Deuteronomy 6:5 Love the Lord your God with all your heart and with all your soul and with all your strength.

Have you ever heard the saying that you are a old soul in a young body. Some have remembered living past life experience. Your soul isn't recording of the past lives we've been through. The soul never dies it lives forever. That is why it's important we live in a righteous life. The life you live here on Earth good or bad is going to be your after life. It is important your perception of the world be a positive one. Look at it this way You are producing a record of how your life is going to be in the next realm. If you want to always be treated with respect just have compassion for others. We were created with the a needs for socialization. We are one soul family. When we are able to live as one collective spirit. That is when we can change the reality of the world. Your soul is an energy that connect you to the divine father. We must believe That we can make a difference to change the vibration. The soul has lived many lifetimes. There comes a time when you have to learn what is your true purpose here on this earth. Stop letting fear confusion your soul of who you really are someone of purpose. Your soul is here to make the universe a beautiful place. Stop being distracted by the events of the world. Focus on who you really are someone of essence. Make a decision to change the vibration of the universe. To something much higher than men!

Head Shepherd
P.O.G.
Loving Ministry

PROVERBS 28:23

He that appreciates a man after words shall find more favour than he that flattereth with tongue.

Good Morning People of God. Appreciation is something we all can do more of. When someone does say something nice or just helps you out, say Thank you! Let them know you appreciated their help. Is that hard to remember to do? I didn't understand this when I was in management. But when I was an employee again, I did understand it. It was something simple. The boss made breakfast for all the workers one day. It was nice of her. Just imagine if I knew back then what I know now, it would have been a wonderful work environment.

We all take it for granted when someone gives us a hand. But if you thank them and recognize them, they will be more willing to help you the next time you need it. Everyone wants that pat on the back and that "atta boy". Think back to when someone recognized you how it made you feel. Just try it. Do something unexpected for someone and see the look of excitement on their face for you appreciating them. If we as a people would do this, the world would be a better place.

Head Shepherd
POG

www.ingramcontent.com/pod-product-compliance
Lightning Source LLC
LaVergne TN
LVHW091627070526
838199LV00044B/976